STRANGE LAND

IN A STRANGE LAND

A STUDENT'S GUIDE TO STUDYING ABROAD

STUDY ABROAD INSTITUTE

Copyright © 2020 Study Abroad Institute

All rights reserved. No part of this publication may be reproduced, distributed, or transmitted in any form or by any means, including photocopying, recording, or other electronic or mechanical methods, without the expressed and prior written permission of the publisher, except in the case of brief quotations embodied in critical reviews and in certain other noncommercial uses permitted by copyright law. For permission requests, write to the publisher, addressed "Attention: Permissions Coordinator," at the address below.

Study Abroad Institute
www.studyabroadinstitute.org
info@studyabroadinstitute.org

ISBN 978-0-9987044-6-3 (print)
ISBN 978-0-9987044-7-0 (ebook)

FIRST EDITION

To the students we caught eating at McDonald's in Italy.

CONTENTS

Part One
Introduction 1
1. Studying? Abroad? 3

Part Two
Benefits & Program Types 9
2. Who Studies Abroad? 11
3. The Benefits of International Education........... 13
4. Which Study Abroad Program Is Best? 17

Part Three
Preparation, Mindset, & Intentions 29
5. Travel Is Work 31
6. You Are Responsible for Your Own Transformation 37
7. Setting Intentions, Goals, and Expectations 49
8. Culture Shock and Cultural Adjustment 59
9. It's Time to Go 73

Part Four
Study Abroad Missteps 79
10. Introduction... 81
11. Neglecting Health 85
12. Getting Distracted 93
13. Forgetting Why You're There 99
14. Not Making Local Friends................ 107
15. Not Learning the Language 119
16. Not Getting Uncomfortable 129
17. Not Cultivating a Sense of Place 133
18. Not Reflecting on the Experience ... 141
19. Home Bashing 149

Part Five
Appendix... 157
20. Money Matters 159
21. Staying Safe 163
22. Packing 167
23. Pay it forward.................................... 169

1. STUDYING? ABROAD?

If you're reading this book, you are either seriously thinking about participating in a study abroad program, have already made the commitment to go, or you are currently abroad but feel unfulfilled and need a little help to make the experience better. Whether you're still flipping through program brochures, packing your bags to go on a trip, or currently in the middle of a study abroad adventure, this book will help you make the most out of your time abroad.

Being in a foreign land is, after all, an important part of studying abroad. And, if we're honest with ourselves, being abroad is often the most attractive part of the prospect. It *is* alluring; it conjures up visions of sipping coffee on a European sidewalk, eating interesting insects on sticks on the backstreets of some Asian metropolis, haggling over exotic goods in a Middle Eastern *souk*, or kicking around a soccer ball on some South American shore. We spend a great deal of time envisioning ourselves abroad, immersed in foreign cultures, visiting the UNESCO World Heritage sites, forming foreign friendships, and being worldly and cosmopolitan.

These exciting goals, however, often take precedence over the "study" portion of studying abroad. Let's face it, "studying" is the least sexy part of the term. How many students actually envision themselves in classrooms of foreign universities listening to lectures? How many actually daydream about the prospect of sitting in intensive language classes struggling to learn new languages? How many fantasize about being shut-in and alone in bedrooms, writing term papers while trying to resist the pressures of enjoying a night on the town? How about cramming for exams in libraries without air conditioning? To be sure, while some of us may have envisioned the "studying" part as central to the experience, it is often the part that we bemoan and, perhaps, view as a deal with the devil that grants us the opportunity to enjoy the otherworldly pleasures of being in a foreign land.

The truth is that the "studying" part is just as important, alluring, and exciting as the "abroad" part. In fact, something interesting happens when the two elements come together. Traveling abroad becomes more meaningful with learning, and learning becomes more efficient and effective while abroad. They combine to make something greater, more powerful, and more rewarding than the sum of their individual parts. Simply put, "studying"—or, more loosely, "learning"—makes the entire experience of traveling more enriching and gratifying.

To give an obvious example, it is easy to imagine all the benefits and efficiencies provided by learning the Italian language in Italy when compared to learning it in Iowa; not only does one learn the language more quickly in Italy, but one learns about Italian history and culture more intimately, to say nothing about all the life skills and so-called "soft skills" gained along the way. You will grow and develop more as an individual by studying a language *in situ* than by listening to podcasts while jogging in your local park.

Another obvious point is that learning doesn't have to be boring or stuffy, and it certainly is not necessarily confined to a lecture hall. Recall that it was Herman Melville who said that the "whale-ship was my Yale College and my Harvard." The point is that learning by doing something is often preferred over learning about how to do something. To put it another way, learning through personal experience is often the best way to learn. And studying abroad offers a great number of experiences that you can learn from, more than what a classroom can provide.

INTRODUCTION 5

A CAVEAT

While there is a great *potential* for you to grow and strive while studying abroad, I've seen many students struggle, get distracted, or generally fail to live up to their potentials. This little book will help you take advantage of your time abroad, enabling you to achieve more, get more out of your experiences, and succeed during and after your program.

This book is not designed to be a handbook of study abroad programs. It doesn't go into detail on how to look for, choose, or pay for programs. It will not provide you with a list of practical traveling tips, like what to pack, how to find local bus schedules, how to decipher the metric system, how to earn income under-the-table, how to open bank accounts, and so on. There are other books that do just that, like Shelley Story's short and accessible *Prepare for Departure* and the thorough and excellent *A Student Guide to Study Abroad* by Stacie Berdan, Allan Goodman, and Cyril Taylor. While my book does briefly touch on fundamental practices of studying abroad in the appendix (safety, packing, money matters, choosing a program, scholarships, etc.), the bulk of the book focuses on what is missing in the other books on the subject of studying abroad. Its aim is to help you cultivate a mindset for success abroad by offering practical and actionable tips to make the most of your experiences. This book will help you understand some of the common roadblocks, obstacles, and *faux pas* students encounter while studying abroad. And it provides strategies on how to overcome or avoid them all together.

It is not necessary to employ every idea in this book to have a successful or meaningful international experience. You can use the ideas piecemeal, adopting the practices, tips, and mindsets that best suit your particular situation and level of comfort. Or, you can simply use this book to identify the common pitfalls so that you can avoid them should they appear before you.

As a professor who leads study abroad programs, I see a pattern of common missteps that students make while studying abroad. But, I was also once a study abroad student myself and experienced the same issues students face today. As the saying goes, "Experience is a tough professor; she gives you the test before the lesson." I wrote this book in hopes that you can learn the lessons gleaned from my observations and experiences before you take the test yourself.

WHO IS THIS BOOK FOR?

Though this book is principally designed to be a preparatory guide for students who haven't yet left for their destinations, many of its lessons will be salient for students in the middle of their experiences and even for students returning for another semester or year abroad. After all, some of the ideas and insights in this book didn't become clear to me until many years after I returned from studying abroad. This book is also for former students who might be participating in long-term programs like the Peace Corps or the various teach-English-abroad programs around the world. Ultimately, this book is as much for the first-time traveler who has never been on an airplane as it is for the students who have been unsatisfied with their experiences abroad. The adult who is moving abroad for work or recreation and needs some tips on how to ensure his or her experience is fulfilling and enriching may also find this book useful. In short, this book is designed for anyone going abroad for an extended period of time.

This book is also designed for travelers of all backgrounds. While the study abroad statistics reveal that most of the students who study abroad are female, white, young, and of a higher socioeconomic status, this book will help students of all ages, races, backgrounds, and genders. If you're in the minority, and by that I mean anyone who isn't white, female, young, and well-to-do, don't let the statistics put you off. In fact, this should excite you. Don't think of yourself as a "minority" or part of an "underrepresented group." Think of yourself, rather, as part of an elite group of individuals, a trailblazer who will be embarking down an untrodden path.

CONGRATULATE YOURSELF

I congratulate you for making the decision to study abroad. Not studying abroad, or not studying abroad sooner, is a common regret adults have. In fact, it is a regret that even long-term travelers have, as revealed to me by Matt Kepnes, founder of nomadicmatt.com and the *New York Times* bestselling author of *How to Travel the World on $50 a Day*. It is also a regret that I have.

I wish I would have studied abroad as an undergrad. My issue was not financial. My issue was immaturity, and I was ignorant of the possibilities and benefits of studying abroad. It is one of the deepest regrets I hold. I traveled abroad often as a child and young adult, but it was on holidays with my parents or to visit family. Travel for me as a child was something that I *had* to do. It took me away from the comforts of my childhood and, therefore, it wasn't something that really excited me. That all changed when, after I had graduated from university, my father invited me to travel to Europe with him. It was then, when I was twenty-something and had just finished my bachelors, that I first enjoyed the liberating and rewarding experiences of international travel. It was then that I first began kicking myself for not having traveled sooner. It was then that I swore to myself that I'd make international travel an important part of my professional and personal life. I was hooked.

I think they call this the "travel bug," and there is a good chance you'll catch it when you travel abroad. The travel bug drove me to take solo trips to parts of the world that scared my parents and, later, to conduct doctoral research in the historical archives in Spain, where I lived and studied for about a year as a graduate student. Now, in my current role as a professor, I lead short-term study abroad programs and even help other professors develop their own international programs. While the same can't be said for other diseases, there is nothing more rewarding than helping spread the "travel bug" affliction.

Part of the joy of being an international educator is seeing how international experiences and studying abroad changes lives. We would love to hear about all of your wonderful experiences and how this book has helped you. Send us an email (info@studyabroadinstitute.org) with stories, pictures, and news of your adventures for a chance to get featured on our website. We look forward to hearing from you. And congratulate yourself for making such a bold move!

Part Two
Benefits &
Program Types

"Broad, wholesome, charitable views of men and things cannot be acquired by vegetating in one little corner of the earth all one's lifetime."

— Mark Twain, *Innocents Abroad*

2. WHO STUDIES ABROAD?

If you study abroad, you'll share company with a very small percentage of global students. According to NAFSA, the Association of International Educators, about 1.5 percent of all students enrolled in institutions of higher education in the United States participate in study abroad programs. In 2016/17, this amounted to around 333,000 students. The statistics in Europe are similar. So, congratulations on your good fortune, and welcome to the club! You will belong to an elite group of students who have had the luck, courage, and privilege to participate in these exclusive experiences.

I use the word "privilege" here conscientiously. As I mentioned earlier, the general profile of students who study abroad is "white, female, young, single, financially comfortable, and without disability." In fact, in 2016/17, over 67 percent of all US study abroad students were female, over 70 percent of all US study abroad students were white, and nearly 92 percent reported no disability. By the way, about two thirds of all study abroad students major in the STEM areas and over 54 percent of US students study abroad in Europe.

That being said, if you diverge from this general profile in any way, if you're a person of color, male or intersex, a minority, economically disadvantaged, have special needs, or wish to pursue a degree not typically associated with international education, studying abroad is not off limits or out of reach. Quite the opposite.

There is an argument to be made about how being in a "minority group" and also studying abroad gives you a distinction others simply do not have. In short, you will be even more special among your peers for pursuing these experiences. Plus, being in the minority also gives you access to a number of special-interest scholarships that will help you fund these experiences. I don't mean to be glib. Rather, I wish to motivate you to rise above personal, professional, or historical inequities. Everyone should have access to these international experiences.

Whether you fall inside or outside of the general profile, you're in rare company, and studying abroad will give you a certain set of tangible and intangible takeaways. To be clear, the mere act of studying abroad will not grant you any skills or insights. On the contrary, it is easy to get distracted while abroad and, as a result, fail to take full advantage of the experience. All the positive benefits are developed by those who spend a significant time abroad and devote themselves to making the most of their experiences. This book will help you do that.

Before we get into the tools you can use to leverage your time abroad into a meaningful set of benefits, we should probably mention what the benefits are and the types of study abroad programs that best cultivate them.

3. THE BENEFITS OF INTERNATIONAL EDUCATION

One of the most popular attractions of studying abroad is cultural and linguistic immersion. And this just so happens to be related to one of the highest self-reported benefits of studying abroad: language acquisition.

In a world in which English is the *lingua franca*, English-speakers who study abroad will have the opportunity to learn another language. If you've spent any time traveling abroad, surely you will have noticed the prevalence of English around the world. My wife, who is French, does not need to learn Spanish before she travels to Latin America, because she can somewhat reliably expect English to suffice. She gets a pass, however, as English is not her mother tongue. But native English-speakers do not, in my opinion, as you earn no favors by expecting others to speak your language when you travel to their country. In many cases, people won't mind; they might, in fact, be happy to practice their English with you. But, studying abroad anywhere outside of the Anglophone world gives you the rare opportunity to immerse yourself in another language and culture and sharpen a skill that many English-speakers find unnecessary or a waste of time.

Some psychologists believe that bilingualism is indicative of a smarter, more perceptive individual. Indeed, a 2012 *New York Times* article boldly reports that being bilingual "makes you smarter." Bilingualism, the article reads, "can have a profound effect on your brain, improving cognitive skills not related to language and even shielding against dementia in old age." These cognitive skills include "a heightened ability to monitor the environment."

To this, some psychologists say that bilingualism increases the propensity to be culturally, socially, and linguistically adaptable; to remember; and to focus attention, and so on.

There are also some "soft skills" one can develop when studying abroad. Living in a globalized world necessitates a greater degree of global-mindedness. And learning a foreign language is one of the signs that an individual might be globally competent. To be sure, students with global competencies are better positioned to succeed in this interconnected environment than students without global skills.

Think about it: if you were a top executive of an American company looking to increase business in Asian markets, who would you hire? The person who studied business in an American university, or the person who studied business in an American university and also spent a year studying international business in China? Who would you hire? The person who has a basic understanding of Mandarin after two semesters in an American university, or the person who has a deeper understanding of Mandarin and Chinese cultural norms after studying in China for a year? The international and global competencies that one gains from studying abroad are among the chief soft skills one can cultivate abroad.

The benefits of studying abroad, however, go well beyond the development of language skills, intercultural skills, and skills that make individuals desirable in the workplace. In fact, academic studies repeatedly illustrate a positive correlation between studying abroad and the cultivation of a variety of *personal* soft skills when compared to individuals who do not study abroad.

According to one 2016 survey of study abroad participants, 92 percent of students "feel they increase their versatility during their stay abroad, meaning they become more resilient, open minded and curious after being abroad and able to adapt to different situations." A large 90 percent of students say they "feel more confident and ready to take on new challenges after their period abroad." Similarly, 87 percent of students "say that their stay abroad made them more tolerant toward other people's values and behaviors" and that they are "now better able to cooperate with people from different backgrounds and cultures." Participants self-report positive transformations like this across the board.

But, as I said earlier, the mere act of studying abroad will not bestow any magical gifts, qualities, or benefits upon you. The benefits you get out of studying abroad must be actively cultivated and earned. Given the wide variety of study abroad programs available, however, some programs are better positioned to help you cultivate those benefits. The next section will help you make sense of the variety of study abroad programs, and it will help you understand which type of program will be most beneficial to you.

The mere act of studying abroad will not bestow any magical gifts, qualities, or benefits upon you. The benefits you get out of studying abroad must be actively cultivated and earned.

4. WHICH STUDY ABROAD PROGRAM IS BEST?

There is a wide variety of study abroad programs available to students, all with their unique set of pros and cons. Not all international programs are made alike. In what follows, I will provide you with an overview of the various kinds of study abroad models, with a few pros and cons for each.

In the name of transparency, prepare for a hard sell that "more is better" in the context of study abroad. In a nutshell, long-term programs have the most impact and are the most beneficial. So, if you are already on a long-term study abroad program or have committed to one, feel free to skip ahead to Part Three.

SHORT-TERM STUDY ABROAD PROGRAMS

Short-term programs are currently the most popular. According to the 2018 Open Doors Report, nearly 65 percent of American students who studied abroad participated in short-term programs. While there is some debate as to what constitutes "short term," a rule of thumb is that short-term programs are those that run for eight weeks or less. Thus, a week-long tour of England and an eight-week summer study in Japan would both qualify as short-term programs. Some people call these programs "study tours," and they are regularly offered at high schools and universities during winter, spring, and summer breaks.

Depending on the school offering the study abroad program, college credit may or may not be available. However, the study abroad programs through academic institutions typically do offer credit. If you are considering a short-term program, it is important to know if it provides academic credit and in what ways the program will help you advance in your degree.

There are many corporations and nonprofit organizations that offer these types of short-term study abroad programs for high schools and universities. They are known as "program providers." The quality and prices vary depending on provider, duration, and location. Some program providers combine student groups from different schools in their international programs, a situation that results in a large group of Americans from different institutions traveling together. In my opinion, this is not ideal, as it is not conducive to providing students with one of the most important goals of studying abroad to begin with: engaging as much as possible with the culture you're visiting.

It is my recommendation that you reconsider short-term study abroad providers that combine their programs with student groups from other schools from around the United States. They're expensive and the quality of experience they provide is a matter of debate.

It is also my recommendation that you reconsider short-term study abroad programs that are not linked to academic credit if you're pursuing a college degree. To be sure, you can learn a lot on these "study tours" that do not offer credit. But you can effectively organize the same program yourself and hire the same local guides for a fraction of the cost and without the frustrations, distractions, and inconveniences that come with traveling within a large group of people from your own country.

There are reasons why short-term programs are popular. They are often more affordable when compared to other types of programs. They also fit nicely into the holidays of the academic year, so you can potentially earn academic credit during breaks and more efficiently work toward your degree in an international environment. Spending a week or two abroad with a group may also be appealing if you have limited travel experience, need more personal or emotional development before spending several months abroad, or are generally intimidated by the prospect of international travel. They can also serve as a "gateway drug," if you will, getting you hooked on exploring the world.

There are some cons of short-term programs. If you were to compare the per-day costs of these short-term programs, you would find that they are far more expensive than the other types of programs I will detail below. Conversely, they are far less beneficial for students when compared to their long-term counterparts. As I will explain below, studies show that the benefits of studying abroad are more visible in those who participate in long-term programs. Short-term programs are also not as ideal for forming lasting connections with locals, learning languages, or cultivating a sense of place in this world.

What's more, while short-term programs are often packed full of learning experiences and activities, participants often report feeling overwhelmed and rushed while visiting important cultural or historical sites, thereby limiting any potential gains or exposure to and engagement with the new culture.

LONG-TERM STUDY ABROAD PROGRAMS

Once far more popular than they are now, long-term programs are semester-long or, better yet, year-long programs. According to the Open Doors Report, 33 percent of American students who studied abroad went on semester-long programs, and 2 percent spent at least one academic year abroad.

There are many nonprofit organizations that offer semester-long study abroad opportunities. Some major American universities have "international campuses" or "study centers" where students live and study for a semester at a time. These programs often offer college credit, as you must attend classes as if you were at your home institution. While the total costs are often much more expensive than short-term programs, the per-day costs are typically much lower, and the benefits are far superior and more numerous. Many smaller colleges and universities partner with study abroad consortia, like the College Consortium for International Studies (CCIS), which help students from smaller institutions connect with larger international universities.

And don't ignore the attainable prospect of studying as an international student enrolled full-time in a foreign university. Studying as an international student independent of any nonprofit organization or business that helps connect you with them takes more time and patience. But the costs of getting a bachelor's degree at an international university are thousands of dollars cheaper than the same degree at an American university, and there are international universities in which the coursework is conducted only in English. To make this option even more appealing, a bachelor's degree in Europe is usually three years instead of the normal four in the United States, thereby increasing the savings.

In any event, study abroad experts agree that long-term programs are better than short-term programs in the cultivation of meaningful experiences and skills. The length of stay makes it easier for students to form lasting relationships with cultures, peoples, and languages.

As you can imagine, long-term programs are far more expensive than short term programs. They also require a greater degree of academic planning. In addition, studying abroad for a year can be intimidating, and being away from family and friends for an extended period of time is often seen as an issue.

TEACHING ENGLISH ABROAD

You don't need to rely on universities to partake in a long-term experience abroad. While technically not "studying abroad," there are opportunities for university graduates to teach English abroad or to become English-language assistants. These are usually paid positions that provide the participant a monthly stipend in order to teach, or help a foreign instructor teach, English to K-12 students.

There are myriad programs all over the world, including some in China, Japan, Korea, Spain, France, and elsewhere. The *Auxiliar de Conversación* program in Spain and the JET program in Japan are a few of the best-known examples. These types of programs are good options for adults and college graduates who have missed the opportunity to study abroad for academic credit but who want to experience the joys and benefits of living abroad.

Programs like these are often paid, and they cultivate deep local connections, language abilities, and intercultural competencies. Some programs call for full-time teaching, while others demand as little as four hours a day. Think of these programs not as vacations, but as contracted international work focused on someone else's learning. Nevertheless, the international teacher of English will undoubtedly learn a great deal and have an immersive experience like no other. The tips in this book will help these types of travelers too.

WHICH STUDY ABROAD PROGRAM IS RIGHT FOR ME?

If you are thinking about studying abroad, and you attend a large university, your first step should be to contact your international education office to talk to the advisers about your options and opportunities. Just don't faint when you see the price tag. As I mentioned earlier, some universities offer in-house study abroad programs at foreign study centers.

Smaller universities and institutions that do not have their own dedicated study abroad offices or foreign study centers sometimes participate in consortia that help send students to foreign universities. These international programs enroll students from a variety of states and countries. In my opinion, these are better than universities' foreign campuses or study centers as your classmates will be more diverse. For instance, the college that I currently work for does not have an international study center, but it works with an organization called CCIS to place students in foreign universities. So, if a student at my college wanted to spend a semester or two studying art history in Italy, they can enroll in the American University of Rome through my college and CCIS.

However, like university study centers, these programs come at a cost. For around $13,000 a semester (not including room and board), students can study at the American University of Rome. Moreover, the student body is not as Italian as it would seem. In 2018, less than 20 percent of the total student population of the American University of Rome were actually Italian.

In my opinion, the most interesting option (and the most difficult) is to attend a foreign university. For the sake of comparison, let's contrast the American University of Rome with a foreign university like the Sapienza Università di Roma. Of course, the American University of Rome is, well, American. Affluent students wishing to get an American-style education will likely enroll at this institution. Your classmates will be mostly wealthy Americans, with the rest being wealthy foreigners from around the world. Courses will be taught in English unless they are foreign-language courses. And at around $25,000 per academic year for tuition alone, not including room and board, the damage to your bank account will rival the damage done by American universities located in the USA. If this is something that appeals to you and your bank account, then by all means go for it. Studying abroad at one of these types of institutions is excellent and, of course, better than not studying abroad at all.

In contrast, however, at the Sapienza Università di Roma, you will have mostly Italian classmates. The courses will be taught in the Italian language. And, thanks to European educational policies, the average tuition for international students in European universities is about $7,000 for the entire year. To be sure, this model has higher risks of homesickness, loneliness, and culture shock. It also has higher demands, like knowing the language and being committed to live in another country without much support. But with high risks come high rewards.

Imagine how many foreign friends you could have. Imagine how many local experiences you could be privy to because of your friends. Imagine how strong your foreign-language skills could become after just one year. Imagine how intimately your knowledge of another country, its people, and yourself could be. Imagine how much money you will save. Who knows? Imagine how you'll meet your future Italian lover.

There are some 350 European schools offering over 1,700 degree programs in the English language. What's more, as Jennifer Viemont tells us, "there are almost 400 programs with tuition less than $4,000 per year and fifty options that are tuition-free—even for international students." And, as I mentioned earlier, bachelor's degrees in Europe take three years to complete instead of four. If you do the math, "it costs less to obtain a full bachelor's degree in Europe, including cost of travel, than ONE year of US out-of-state or private school tuition." For an excellent book that focuses on this option, see Jennifer Viemont's *College Beyond the States: European Schools That Will Change Your Life Without Breaking the Bank.*

The point is that the more local the program, the more opportunities for growth and reward you will have. Ultimately, you'll need to assess your personal background, levels of commitment and adventurousness, and financial resources to determine which program is best for you.

SEVEN DIMENSIONS TO A STUDY ABROAD PROGRAM

In a recent article, Lilli and John Engle break down the different types of study abroad programs. They classify them into five types.

Type One: Study Tour
Type Two: Short-Term Study
Type Three: Cross-Cultural Contact
Type Four: Cross-Cultural Encounter
Type Five: Cross-Cultural Immersion

The Engles' classification system depends on the answers to the following questions: How long is the program? How much of the local language do you need to know before entering the program? Are the classes conducted in English or in the foreign language of the country hosting the program? Are your classmates foreigners and locals alike, or just foreigners like you? Do you live with other foreigners or with a local host family? Are you required to take part in cultural projects and programs? Is there an adviser to help you adjust and ensure that you're making the most of the experience?

The Engles developed a sliding scale for seven criteria and concluded that, from Study Tours to Cross-Cultural Immersions, we see the following trends: 1) the program duration increases, 2) the foreign language requirements become more demanding, 3) the number of classes taught in the foreign language increases, 4) classmates are more and more local, 5) the housing situation shifts from student groups belonging to the same, home culture living in dorms to homestays with foreign families, 6) there are increasing requirements to participate in cultural projects and programs, and 7) the amount and quality of guidance shift from simple orientation programs to ongoing checkups and advising.

As you can tell, there is a wide variety of programs to suit the individual needs of each student. But a good rule of thumb for having a fulfilling, immersive, and rewarding experience abroad is to join a program on the higher end of the chart. In other words, the most beneficial and difficult study abroad programs are ones that are long-term, require an understanding and a daily use of local languages, enroll predominantly local students, set students up with host families, require regular cultural interaction, and ensure regular student advising and reflection. No program is perfect, so it is best to see where you feel most comfortable on the scale for each criterium.

MY RECOMMENDATION

I strongly recommend that students take part in long-term study abroad experiences, ones that last at least a semester but preferably two. If you are undecided about which program to choose, or are currently in the phase of selecting programs, then I recommend that you consider participating in a year-long program or, at the very least, a semester-long program instead of a short-term program lasting two weeks or less. As I have already alluded to, research shows that the student obtains more benefits from the experience of a long-term program when compared to a short-term one.

That being said, even short-term programs can be transformative. I highly recommend that you enroll in a short-term program *if* a long-term program is out of reach for whatever reason. However, before giving up your dreams to take part in a long-term study abroad program due to financial concerns, please research scholarships.

Speak with a study abroad adviser at a local university to help you find scholarships and grants, as millions of dollars are available each year to help students without financial resources grow and develop as global citizens (see "Money Matters" in the Appendix for more information). And finally, if you're American, don't forget to calculate the costs of a four-year program in the United States against the costs of a three-year program in Europe. You may find that getting an education in a European university is cheaper in the long run, to say nothing of its being more rewarding.

※

The percentage of students who have enriching experiences abroad and who develop important global competencies and international skills is quite low. If you participate in a study abroad program, you'll be in rarefied company. You'll be in the 2 percent of total students who have the opportunities to develop hard and soft skills and have transformative experiences. When leveraged correctly, you can use your study abroad experience to your future advantage, to help you grow socially, professionally, creatively, and personally. This book will help you get the most out of your experiences abroad so that you can do just that. It will help you figure out your own goals and help you make the most out of your time abroad.

As I mentioned earlier, it is important to understand that the benefits of studying abroad do not magically appear just because you happen to be studying in a foreign country. You must actively cultivate and develop them. In short, you need to be clear in your goals and motivations and put in the time and effort. In the next section of this book, you will identify your intentions, interests, and goals in order to formulate a plan to explore and achieve them.

REFLECT

1. Consider the pros and cons of both short- and long-term programs. Does one type of program appeal to you more? Why?
2. If you are not interested in a long-term program, list the reasons why. Are there barriers preventing you from studying abroad longer? If so, can they be overcome? What course of action would you need to take to be able to participate in a long-term program?
3. In what ways do you think studying abroad will help you become a better individual, student, citizen, or employee?
4. What parts of the world would you like to study abroad in? Why? Can you identify specific countries or more specific regions? And can you narrow it down to individual cities? Do some research and think about what each one of your top cities offers and how studying there could help advance your life and career.
5. Why do you want to study abroad? What do you want to get out of it?

Part Three
Preparation, Mindset, & Intentions

"I don't like work—no man does—but I like what is in the work—the chance to find yourself."

– Marlow, in Joseph Conrad's *Heart of Darkness*

5. TRAVEL IS WORK

The plane landed in Frankfurt at 8:00 a.m. local time, which meant it was 2:00 a.m. back home. Being awake at 2:00 a.m. wasn't anything unusual for me; in fact, it wasn't unusual for me to still be at a bar at that hour. But this felt different. I was beat down not by loud music, booze, and secondhand smoke, but by roaring engines, bland food, and the airplane's dry air. I thought I would be able to get some sleep on the plane, but I quickly understood that to be a terrible assumption after a restless mother and a crying toddler took their seats next to me. To make matters worse, the teenager sitting behind me, who was playing a fierce game of *Bejeweled* on the seatback entertainment system, kept hitting my seat. The transatlantic flight sapped my energy and tested my limits.

And now, I had less than an hour to rush through customs and immigration and make my connecting flight. I pulled my carry-on through the queue of people in the non-EU passports line. I had a connecting flight I simply couldn't afford to miss, I told them, so I elbowed and apologized my way through the gauntlet of leering eyes and sarcastic responses. "You're not the only one here in a rush," was a common refrain.

I made it through immigration with my passport stamped and my ego battered, but what awaited me on the other side would test my resolve even more. My connecting flight to Paris had been delayed. With suddenly two more hours to kill, I walked laps around the terminal, smelled the entire collection of duty free cologne, and ignored the smartass who, when he walked by, mumbled, "I thought you were in a rush."

I eventually boarded the plane, and no sooner had I closed my eyes than the plane landed in Paris. I collected my bags and learned that the buses that took travelers from the airport to the center of town weren't running. The drivers were on strike. The airport Wi-Fi wasn't working, and I had no mobile data on my phone to research alternative routes to downtown. I walked to the taxi line demoralized, cursing, and worried that the taxi driver would take me on the "scenic route" through the French countryside. How would I even know he wasn't taking the most direct route?

In the best French I could muster, I asked about the fare and told the taxi-driver where I was going. "A Pigalle," I said, and we peeled away from the airport and wove through traffic as if the driver were racing in the 24 Hours of Le Mans. A broken man with an aching body and frazzled nerves, I arrived, forty euros later, at my hostel, where, that night, I had one of the best nights of sleep I've ever had.

Stories like the one above happen every day on every continent. They are not unusual or atypical travel experiences. But they can be physically and emotionally challenging for the new and experienced traveler alike.

The word "travel" comes from the Old French word *travaillier* and is related to the English word "travail," both of which literally mean "to suffer, to be worn out." Today, the modern French words for "work" and "to work" are *travail* and *travailler*, respectively.

The word "travel" arrived in the English language with the meaning "to go on a journey" as early as the thirteenth century. Then, however, the word also held connotations of difficulty and inconvenience. This makes sense. Imagine the amount of time, energy, and resources that it took our medieval ancestors to travel from town to town. Imagine the dangers and pitfalls that pilgrims endured along their routes. Imagine the treacheries of the road: brigands, pirates, storms, wild animals. Indeed, even earlier in history, consider the ancient epics like *The Odyssey* and *The Aeneid*, which told the stories of heroes overcoming fantastic obstacles and hardships while on their journeys. While modern technology and engineering has certainly made travel more comfortable, it is, and will likely always remain, hard work that stresses both the body and mind.

The word "vacation" is almost as old as the word "travel." One of the earliest examples of this word is found in Chaucer's well-known *The Canterbury Tales*, in which the Wife of Bath's fifth husband, Jankyn, is described as reading a book "When he had leisure and vacation / From other worldly occupation." The implication here being that a vacation is something unrelated to work or "worldly occupations"; rather, it is a moment of rest and relaxation.

A vacation, then, is the very opposite of work in this early formulation. Indeed, a vacation begins as soon as the work ends. And this implication makes sense given the word "vacation" is related to words like "vacuum," "vacuous," "vacancy," and "vacate." It is related to being free from something and being empty.

This appears to be the model upon which the major cruise lines and so-called "all inclusive" resorts operate. They take care of all the details from the itinerary and planned excursions and activities to food and drink. Everything is carefully orchestrated for you to think and worry as little as possible, as if you were floating around in a closed-off bubble, comfortable and amused. However, like a bubble, vacations are often not filled with anything substantial or weighty, especially when compared to travel.

Many astute travelers consider modern forms of vacation to be the very opposite of travel. This is not to say that spending quality time with family and friends or having mindless fun is meaningless or unimportant. But *travel* is different and gives travelers the opportunity for growth and reward in exchange for the hardships they endure. It can be something that transforms the mind.

My brain had shut down. I had considered myself fluent in Spanish, but after an entire day of speaking, reading, and listening to Spanish at an academic conference in Madrid, I felt as if I were in a high school Intro to Spanish course, barely cobbling together poorly conjugated sentences and placing o's and a's at the ends of English words as if it would magically transform them into Spanish. Like a muscle that fails during an intense exercise, my brain had simply given up. And there I was, in front of a professor whose research I had read and admired, in front of the only person with whom I wanted to share my own research, and the words just stopped.

In hindsight, what I had experienced was mental fatigue. I was simply overstimulated. People who are multilingual or are learning a new language will know what I'm talking about. As it does to the body, travel often presents opportunities that overstimulate and test the limits of the mind.

Travel challenges the mind cognitively and psychologically. To be sure, you'll overload your senses being in new social situations, seeing new sights, and hearing new sounds. Just recall how quickly your energy flags when you're studying. Mental overload is real and doesn't happen just to introverts like me.

It is helpful to think about these two ideas—travel and vacation—from an intellectual perspective. In travel, one's mind is often "at work." During a vacation, however, one's mind is comparatively "empty." A vacationer seems to be more like someone who sips a piña colada at a beachside resort than a traveler who, conversely, seems to be more like someone who visits museums or goes on historical walking tours through ancient ruins.

Travelers are mentally engaged, learn, reflect on their experiences, and make lasting connections with people. Vacationers undergo periods of mental and physical rest; a traveler does not.

Again, there is nothing wrong with vacations. It is often beneficial to schedule periods of rest in order to "recharge" and grow, but it is important to see the differences in approach.

How does all this relate to studying abroad? I want you to think of your time studying abroad as travel, not as a vacation. Simply put, studying abroad is travel in the proper sense of the term. It is not a vacation. Studying abroad requires a great deal of physical, mental, and emotional work.

Studying abroad, when done right, helps strengthen the mind. It is mentally exhausting, not just because of the stress of physical difficulties but because of learning and mental stimulation. Receptive individuals will engage in the study abroad experience with their eyes and mind opened, curious and ready to absorb as much as possible. The engaged traveler has a mind that is constantly "switched on," experiencing, engaging, reflecting, and learning.

While both notions of travel and vacationing might be fun and pleasurable, it is travel that supplies the biggest opportunities for transformation and reward. This is why, paradoxically perhaps, many people enjoy the more demanding act of traveling; that somehow, amid the stress, difficulties, and issues—amid the delays, crying babies, and mental breakdowns—there is something profoundly rewarding about it all.

REFLECT

1. Have you ever been bored while visiting a new place? Was it a time of relaxation, or was it a time of mental and physical activity? What could you have done to make it even more personally enriching?
2. In what ways can travel be difficult? How can you transform difficulties and hardships on the road into positive and rewarding experiences?
3. Which common travel situations give you mental stress? Which give you physical discomfort? If you've never traveled, try to imagine scenarios that might easily stress you. What could you do to anticipate and mitigate these stressful or demanding situations?
4. In what ways might you enhance a family vacation to make it more meaningful?

6. YOU ARE RESPONSIBLE FOR YOUR OWN TRANSFORMATION

I didn't know him for very long, not even an entire year, but I felt as if I had known Eric since childhood. He was friendly, outgoing, and intellectually curious. But something was wrong that day when we met at a neighborhood café in Seville. He was thinking about leaving halfway through his yearlong program. It caught me off guard.

"Are you serious? What's going on?" I asked, bewildered.

"I don't know, man," Eric said. "I know it is weird to say this, but I feel bored."

"You're bored? Here? How could you possibly be bored? And here of all places? Look around you! There are beautiful women here, cheap beer, and deep history."

"Yeah, man. I know it sounds weird. I love this place. It just feels like something is missing."

"What do you mean?"

"I don't know. I thought Spain would be this wonderful change. That it would present opportunities for me to basically reinvent myself. But it is the same crap, different country."

Eric didn't have negative things to say about anyone or anything in Spain in particular, which suggested that he wasn't suffering from culture shock (more on this later). But he revealed to me that he was feeling just as unfulfilled as he had felt before leaving the United States.

I understood. Feeling unfulfilled in the United States was one of the motivating factors for me to leave. But it seemed like Eric was putting too much hope in Spain to resolve his issues for him. It was as if he were entirely dependent upon the external world for finding meaning in his experience, as if he were expecting Spain to give him things, instead of expecting to take things away from his time in Spain.

The mere act of traveling abroad and changing your environment is not enough to bring meaning and fulfillment into your life. This, of course, is the argument the Roman philosopher Seneca makes in one of his letters to his friend. Quoting Socrates, Seneca tells his friend that travel alone will not cure his problems or give him meaning, because "you always take yourself with you." Later, in another letter, Seneca advises his friend that "you need not another place, but another personality." Travel may temporarily distract you from unhappiness or discontent, but "the reasons that set you wandering are ever at your heels." And this is one of the takeaways of Elizabeth Gilbert's famous memoir, *Eat, Pray, Love*. A change of scenery, even a tour around the world, can only do so much to satisfy the soul.

※

The professor had asked the class to read an essay by the French philosopher Jean Paul Sartre entitled "Existentialism is a Humanism." The essay's atheistic premise would challenge my more conservative classmates. But the professor urged us all to look beyond the essay's premise and asked us to consider whether the essay was empowering or not. Considering and understanding a position without blindly accepting it or categorically shutting it down is an important critical-thinking skill to possess, we were urged. So, later that night, I curled up on my couch with a warm tea and read the essay.

I found the essay, published in 1946 and one of Sartre's most famous, to be extremely empowering. Originally given as a lecture and not intended to be a proper philosophical treatment, it is an easy read. But the substance of the essay, not its style or particular delivery, was the most appealing part. I'm not a philosopher or an expert on the topic, but

Sartre's main point was that humans have no overarching and preconceived purpose, fate, or destiny. Because humans are born into the world without any preconceived purposes, we have the responsibility to define ourselves and determine our own purposes. And our definitions of ourselves, who we are and what we become, depend not on our ideas but on our actions. To put it another way, our values are determined by what we do, and not by what we think or say.

What I find convincing and empowering is the humanistic element. Namely, we have within ourselves a great deal of power to form and fashion our own purposes and meanings in this world. This is not an atheistic or new argument; it was argued from a Christian perspective since at least as early as the Renaissance. But, it was this essay that first helped me realize a few things that I thought I had always known: I am responsible for my own successes and failures, that who I become would be the result of my own actions, and that I define myself. If my life is a failure or a success, it will be because of my actions or inactions. Nothing more, nothing less.

Admittedly, this argument is not without some problems. Not everyone can be whatever he or she wants to become in the world. For example, Sartre's argument doesn't take into consideration how cooperation, privilege, and oppression can influence the conditions of someone's life. But the general premise stands mostly true, that you are empowered, given your specific set of constraints and contexts, to define your life's purpose and meaning. And this is something we all already implicitly understand, for if we didn't believe that we had the power to improve our conditions and transform the courses of our lives, why would we go to school to develop skills or learn anything at all?

You might be asking yourself, *What does this have to do with studying abroad and international travel? I didn't sign up for a philosophy lesson!*

The connection is that if you're in an international program, you are presented with a unique opportunity to define yourself, to develop yourself, and even to reinvent yourself through your actions and inactions abroad. Do you want to be someone who merely reminisces about "that one time I studied abroad," or do you want to be someone who is transformed by the experience, becomes intimately engaged in a global context with a near-native intercultural fluency? Do you want to be someone who took advantage of and owned your experience abroad, or do you want to be someone like my friend Eric who was unfulfilled, lost, and searching for external validation?

※

The success or failure of your study abroad experience, in large part, depends on you.

Of course we cannot always control everything in our lives. Our lives' circumstances are often beyond our control. Your housing situation abroad might become less than ideal. You might have a terrible teacher. You might come to find that you dislike the weather in the city you live in. Your classmates may be unfriendly. Your roommates might be incompatible. But what is under your control is how you deal with situations, what you do to make the most of your experiences, and how you overcome adversity.

Work toward cultivating a habit of self-realization, for—if we are to agree with Sartre—you are defined by the sum of your actions and experiences. If you spend your time during your study abroad experience growing, learning languages, and expanding your horizons, then you might just become a scholar, a polyglot, or perhaps a citizen of the world.

Long-term study abroad experiences provide students with the opportunity to take Sartre's argument to heart and to think deeply about self-development and self-realization. Think about it.

What better time to reinvent yourself than during a year-long international program, where you'll be in a new environment and surrounded by people who know very little, if anything, about you and your past. Your life will be like a blank canvas upon which you can begin painting a new portrait of yourself. Heck, you can even go by another name.

The point is not to be deceptive or to abandon your past. You're not James Bond or Jason Bourne, so don't think about creating an alter ego or try to be a mysterious secret agent. But you will have the opportunity and the space to reevaluate your goals, dreams, and desires in life, and begin taking action on them without the typical constraints and naysayers that you might have encountered back home. Simply put, you can begin cultivating a new sense of self.

After all, you will be having new experiences and, if you're traveling alone and have some serious time for reflection and introspection, you will be learning a lot more about yourself than you have ever learned. In your quest of self-discovery, which is one of the great enterprises of studying abroad, you will have the opportunity to follow your dreams, your passions, and your whims.

This is why, quite often, students report returning home from long-term study abroad programs feeling as if they'd become a "new person," with a new approach to life, a new set of skills, and a new understanding about themselves and their place in the world. If you begin a long-term program with this mindset of growth, opportunity, and self-development, you'll likely be radically transformed by the experience. Or, to put it another way, you will take advantage of the experience and transform yourself.

HOW TO HAVE A FULL SET OF EXPERIENCES TO MAXIMIZE YOUR TIME ABROAD

I want you to think about the ways in which you can have fulfilling, rewarding, and successful experiences while studying abroad. I also want you to think about what you want to get out of this experience. Don't worry! This isn't a contract, and it is okay if you do not have a clear idea about this now. But hopefully, after you're done reading this chapter and answering the questions below, your ideas will start coming into focus.

I have identified five dimensions to a fulfilling and successful study abroad experience. Students studying abroad who try to engage in each one of these dimensions will ultimately have a more enriching experience abroad. The five dimensions are *culture, health, academics, social interaction,* and *expression and creativity*. What do these mean? Let me explain.

The *cultural* dimension deals with exploring the host country's history, culture, and society. Why study abroad if you're not going to explore the culture in which you're living? The *health* dimension is one that is not inherent to studying abroad, but should be considered necessary because the study abroad experience is rendered more difficult with an unfit body and mind. The *academic* dimension is the "study" portion of "studying abroad" and deals with areas like learning, study, and career development. The *social* dimension deals with cultivating real friendships abroad and a sense of community. Lastly, the *expression* dimension deals with pursuing creative endeavors.

I've developed an acronym to help you remember the areas: CHASE. I will give more concrete examples of what you can do to engage in the five areas later, but for the time being, here are the areas broken down further:

- <u>Culture</u>: language learning, cultural immersion, travel and exploration
- <u>Health</u>: mental health, physical health
- <u>Academics</u>: career development, discipline enrichment, studying, internships
- <u>Social</u>: friendships, community, networking, relationship building
- <u>Expression</u>: creativity, hobbies

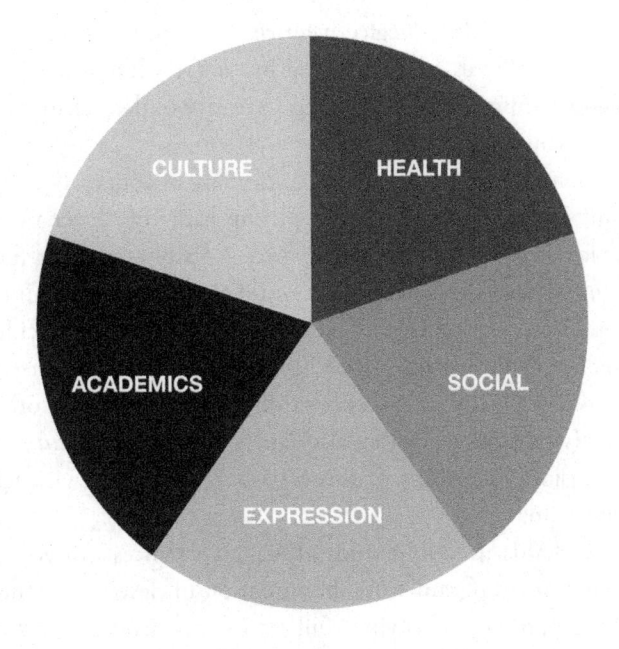

Having a fulfilling and complete study abroad experience requires that you actively engage in these dimensions. It is important to commit a little bit of your time to each one of these main categories every week. Why would you travel to a foreign country to study abroad if you're only going to lock yourself in a library all day and night, and not explore the local culture and the city you're living in? Conversely, why would you travel to a foreign country and enroll in a foreign university if you're not going to reap the benefits of actually studying? Why wouldn't you also want to meet new people and engage in what the area has to offer?

You will no doubt notice that a few of the dimensions might seem like they have little to do with studying abroad or cultural immersion, for instance, the dimensions of *health, social interaction,* and *expression.* However, because you will be living in a foreign land for an extended period of time, you shouldn't neglect *yourself.* You will be unfulfilled and miserable if you're not healthy, you're without a sense of community, or you're lacking a creative outlet, no matter where you are on the planet.

Some of the dimensions can overlap, of course. For example, if you participate in a pickup game of soccer with the locals at a municipal field, you're probably satisfying the *health* dimension. But the case could also be made that it is a *social* or *cultural* activity. While it is up to you to decide which activity satisfies which dimension, challenge yourself not to double dip. If soccer best fulfills *health,* try to do other activities that week that also satisfy the *social* and *cultural* dimensions, like going to dinner with new friends or visiting a museum.

CHASE after your study abroad experiences and goals. Begin your program with the intention of developing and taking part in a satisfying, full set of experiences in what will likely be the prime of your life. As we have already discussed, you are responsible for making the most out of your experiences.

What types of activities can you do to satisfy each CHASE dimension? Here is a list of examples:

- <u>Culture</u>: museums, historical tours, language study, festivals, shows, music, gastronomy
- <u>Health</u>: exercise, meditation, yoga, walking, running, sports, physical therapy
- <u>Academics</u>: studying, internships, conferences, seminars, mentorship relationships
- <u>Social</u>: dinners, community service, team sports, dancing, socializing
- <u>Expression</u>: journaling, photography, writing, painting, playing instruments, creative hobbies

Do not overwhelm yourself. That's not the point. However, do commit to fulfilling at least one activity for each dimension every week. It is not hard to do. If you're studying abroad, chances are that you will attend class, study, and speak with advisers. Chances are, you'll go out with friends to a pub or a nightclub. In doing so, you've already satisfied two dimensions. Surely you have time for visiting a museum, going for a run, and writing in your journal during the week. If you do, you've satisfied all five dimensions.

It sounds simplistic, and it is, but I want you to challenge yourself, to push yourself beyond going for the easy, low-hanging fruit. Of course you'll be studying, but what more can you do to engage academically? Of course you'll be hanging out with your friends, but what different types of social activities can you do? Of course you'll be experiencing a new culture, but what can you do to engage more with it?

A full set of experiences does not mean you should expect to always be stimulated or amazed. In fact, you should expect to be bored or lonely from time to time, just as you were back home. You should expect to have strange, weird, and annoying encounters with people, just as you did in your hometown.

Studying abroad is not a magical experience where mundane drudgery and the quotidian aspects of life cease to exist. You will need to shop for groceries, clean your space, pay bills, and run errands, just as you did back home. You will still need to take out the trash, go to the grocery store, and—hopefully—clean your toilet.

What's changed is the environment in which you do these mundane tasks, so try to approach the mundane with a fresh set of eyes and with the understanding that, though mundane, hidden joys can be found within the new world you're exploring. For example, I find that there is something exciting and wonderful about going into a grocery store in a foreign country. The differences in food often delight and surprise me. Indeed, I can spend hours in a foreign market. I chalk this up as a cultural experience and an opportunity to learn the language and culture of the country I'm visiting. In a new place, everyday experiences can be seen as extraordinary.

You just need to have the right mindset to capitalize on the breadth of your experiences, to have the right goals and intentions, and to understand what kind of opportunities you will have in order to satisfy each dimension, all of which happens to be the subject of the next chapter.

REFLECT

1. What does your ideal life look like? How can your study abroad experience help you cultivate it?
2. What do you dislike about yourself? Do you have any bad habits that you want to break? How can your study abroad experience help you break them? How can study abroad help you change and grow?
3. What do you want to be known for? How can studying abroad help you achieve your goals?
4. What are your hobbies? How can you practice them when you're in another country?
5. Consider creating a pie chart, like the one above, in your journal and coloring-in each one of the dimensions at least once a week. Alternatively, map out your week in your calendar so that you have each dimension's activity planned ahead of time.

"As long as you are ignorant of what you should avoid or seek, or of what is necessary or superfluous, or of what is right or wrong, you will not be traveling, but merely wandering. There will be no benefit to you in this hurrying to and fro." – Seneca, *Letters to Lucilius*

7. SETTING INTENTIONS, GOALS, AND EXPECTATIONS

After moving to Seville, I was invited to a meet-and-greet for *auxiliares*, the term used for those who help professors teach English in Spain. Not one for large and forced social gatherings, I reluctantly went under the pretense that it would be helpful to get to know other newly transplanted Americans like me. As expected, the event felt awkward.

I felt like a fish out of water. It was my first year abroad, and most of the other participants were ten years younger than me and already on their second tour abroad. To be fair, I was well into my doctoral dissertation, and most weren't even thinking about starting their master's degrees yet, but I couldn't help but feel old and inexperienced. Everyone was young, bright-eyed, and optimistic for the future. Me? Old, surly, bitter, and trying to catch a buzz so the experience would be tolerable.

With a glass of wine in hand, I made my rounds asking and answering the same question: "So, why did you decide to come to Spain?"

I eventually met Samantha, a young woman who was assigned to be an *auxiliar* in a city not too far from Seville.

"So, what brings you to Spain?" she asked.

"I'm here to do dissertation research in the archives," I said, for what seemed to be the hundredth time that night. I explained my research to her. Her eyes glazed over. I shifted the conversation to her. "What about you?"

"I'm here with my friends. We all got placed in the same city."

"Cool," I said. "Is there anything you want to see or do here?"

"Well, to be honest, I don't know that much about Spain."

"So, did you study education? Do you want to be a teacher?"

"I'm not sure yet, actually. This seemed like it would be a good chance to check out a new country and figure out what I want to do with my life. And also to have some fun."

After making my rounds, I realized her motivations for moving to Spain were quite common. I found that some of the most common reasons for becoming a teaching assistant in Spain were "I want to have an experience" and "I'm trying to figure out what to do with my life."

To be fair, being an English assistant is quite different from studying abroad in an international program. And taking time off for mental clarity or to just let loose is important. Not everyone has everything figured out, and that's okay. But I've come to learn that the international experience is infinitely more rewarding and enriching, whether studying abroad or teaching abroad, when one has a clear set of goals and motivations for doing so.

Why is this so? Students who have clear goals and motivations prior to travel have a higher rate of success in their study abroad programs. It seems like a no-brainer, but the truth of the matter is that people who are clear in articulating their goals and intentions are more effective in realizing their goals.

It is for this reason that you might want to think about setting goals within the five dimensions of experience I identified in the previous chapter.

Below is a quick breakdown of each dimension to help you think about setting some goals related to each one.

CULTURE

Learning about new cultures is an integral component of studying abroad. Ask yourself, *what can I do to maximize my exposure to the culture while abroad?* Will you explore the country's cuisine, dance, language, music, history, and customs? How will you actually ensure that you explore these areas? Will you take classes, attend festivals, visit museums? What can you do to integrate more deeply into the social fabric of your town or city?

HEALTH

Do not neglect the health of your mind and body no matter where you are. This is especially true when you're out of your cultural element. What specific activities can you do that will help you care for your mental and physical wellbeing? Does your institution offer yoga classes, meditation sessions, or intramural sports? Are there any pickup sports offered in your area? Do you envision yourself hiking or running? Can you join any team sports? Consider setting goals or, at least, observing a schedule that accommodates the habits of a healthy lifestyle.

ACADEMIC

In what ways can you ensure that your travel experience involves the greatest number of opportunities for learning? This question might be answered best if you know exactly what you want to study. While many students will have an "undecided" or "undeclared" major, knowing this information ahead of time will help you understand how the international experience will strengthen your learning. What I mean is, if you know you want to major in a specific field of study, you can design your study abroad experience to help you advance your academic career.

What goals can you set for yourself academically? What can you specifically do during your time abroad to enhance the academic experience? What kind of extracurricular programs does your host institution or country offer? And how could you fit them into your academic schedule? Are there any short-term educational tours into nearby cities, regions, or countries offered by your school during long weekends, breaks, and holidays?

Think about the ways in which your study abroad experience can help you achieve your career goals. What concrete skills can you learn while abroad? What kind of connections can you make in your area or industry? Are there any internship opportunities abroad? Are there any networking opportunities in your field?

If you don't know exactly what you want to do with your life, which is quite okay, think about learning skills that could be generally beneficial to your intellectual development.

SOCIAL

Everyone needs to blow off some steam from time to time. It may seem strange for a professor to encourage students to make goals for downtime or nonacademic fun, but it is important. You don't want to burn out while you're abroad. You should view your international experience as a marathon, not a sprint, so taking your time—and making some time for fun—is of vital importance.

I'm sure you don't need to plan to have some fun abroad. I am equally sure that you probably don't need to schedule or make goals for having fun. But in the event that you're a workaholic, an introvert, or generally antisocial, it is helpful to push yourself to meet new people. Social goals could involve making local friendships, exploring the local food and bar scene, taking cooking classes with friends, or finding a travel buddy to explore new places with.

EXPRESSION

Expression is all about creativity. And as Chase Jarvis puts it, "creativity is the new literacy." What goals can you make that are related to your creative pursuits and hobbies? For example, instead of learning about the local music or cuisine, consider actually learning how to play the music or make the cuisine. You could start a blog about the restaurants or historical sites in your city. You could learn the local dance, take photography courses, or learn how to create a local craft. You could write about your experiences in your university's student newspaper. What are some of the possibilities that align with your interests and location?

ARTICULATING GOALS

One of the most insightful methods in articulating and achieving goals is to remember that you should set SMART goals. The acronym "SMART" is a fashionable mnemonic device to help you remember the important elements of goal setting.

The idea of setting SMART goals was first articulated in the early 1980s and has since caught on. While there are variations, SMART generally stands for Specific, Measurable, Achievable, Realistic, and Timely. Let's break down what each one means.

Specific goals are clear, precise, and singular. A good goal isn't one that is compounded of many variables or achievements. Likewise, a good goal is one that is not vague. For example, learning how to play the guitar seems like a specific goal, but it is vague, as there is a wide variety of levels of skill and styles of guitar playing. Technically speaking, someone who has learned how to play a simple chord on the guitar has "learned how to play the guitar," right? Vague phrases like "learning how to play the guitar" have implications that vary from person to person. Some might suggest this involves a high level of proficiency. Some may, however, suggest that this implies a basic knowledge of guitar fundamentals. Learning the basics of flamenco guitar is a more specific goal, as it focuses on a style and a skill level. Make extremely specific goals.

Measurable goals are goals about which you are able to know whether or not—yes or no—you succeeded in achieving them. Because the point of making goals is to achieve them, being able to measure your progress is important. Will there be a point where you are able to say without a doubt that you've learned how to play the guitar? Many master guitar players make a habit of practicing every day, which illustrates the point that vague and unmeasurable goals like "learn the guitar" or "master the guitar" are ever elusive. Articulate goals that can be measured.

Actionable goals have clear steps that you can take to achieve them. Is achieving the goal dependent on you and your actions, or are they dependent on the actions of others? For instance, "getting a scholarship to study guitar" may not be actionable, as getting a scholarship is, in part, dependent on contingencies beyond your control. "Applying for a scholarship" is better in this respect, as the act of applying depends on you alone. Moreover, is there a clear set of steps over a long term that you can take to work toward achieving your goals? For example, taking weekly guitar lessons or practicing for at least thirty minutes each day are positive actions one can take to achieve a goal. Formulate goals that depend on you taking concrete steps.

Realistic goals are those that are within your power to achieve. For instance, is it realistic to believe that you will be able to develop guitar skills that rival Eric Clapton's in a few months? Realistic goals are goals that are down-to-earth and reasonable. They're not lofty goals that shoot for the stars. It is, of course, arguably good practice to shoot for the stars from time to time, but it isn't good practice in setting SMART goals. Be honest and realistic with yourself.

Finally, *Timely* goals have concrete deadlines. By when would you like to achieve the goals you set? Set yourself a realistic deadline or series of deadlines for the attainment of your goals.

Let's give an example of a SMART goal using the example of guitar playing.

I will learn how to play the twelve-bar blues progression on guitar by the end of the month by taking a blues guitar class and practicing every day for at least thirty minutes.

This goal has all the hallmarks of a SMART goal. It is singular, specific, measurable, actionable, realistic, and sets a specific deadline.

A SHORT WORD ON ACCOUNTABILITY

One helpful technique in achieving goals is to make yourself accountable. There are a variety of ways of ensuring accountability, but common ones are as follows: Write down your goals. Announce your goals to your friends and families. Post your goals on social media. Post your goals on the walls of your bedrooms so you see them every day. Keep a journal and track your progress. Set reminders on your smart phone. Techniques like these are particularly helpful if you lack motivation or get distracted and sidetracked easily.

REFLECT

1. Write out a list of your motivations for studying abroad.
2. Make a list of all the things you want to experience, taste, see, and hear that will advance and deepen your exposure to the host country's culture.
3. Make a list of all the things you foresee yourself doing that will help you stay healthy, both mentally and physically, while abroad.
4. Make a list of all the things you can experience, read, see, do, study, visit, that will advance your academic goals while abroad. This could be for a class you're taking or to simply get ahead in your major. Or, make a list of all the potential opportunities to "pad your resume" while abroad. What career skills can you develop? Are there any volunteer or internship opportunities?
5. Make a list of all the things you could do for fun. What types of things can you foresee yourself doing socially?
6. Make a list of all the things you can do for your creativity. Research to see if there are any local groups in your host country or city.
7. What courses are you taking while studying abroad? What can you do before and during your stay to ensure that you learn as much course content as possible while abroad? For example, if you are planning on taking an art history course while studying in France, what can you do beforehand to make the most out of your future experience? Will you read books on the subject of French art history? Once you are in France, will you visit local art museums?
8. This is the hard part. Compile a list of five goals, one for each CHASE category represented by reflections 2–6, and make each one of them SMART.

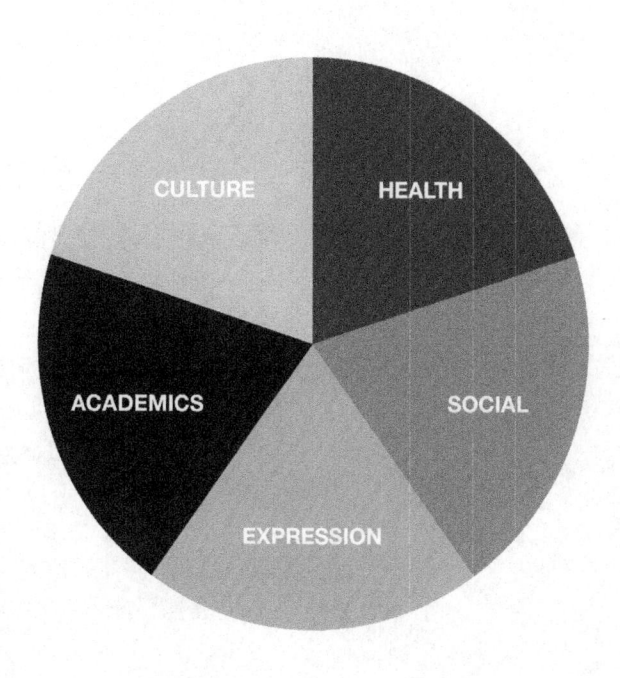

CULTURE

HEALTH

ACADEMICS

SOCIAL

EXPRESSION

"Travel does not make a physician or an orator; no art is acquired by merely living in a certain place."

— Seneca, *Letters to Lucilius*

8. CULTURE SHOCK AND CULTURAL ADJUSTMENT

At the *auxiliar* meet-and-greet I also met a guy named Jason who was embarking on his first year abroad. Being that we were assigned to teaching English at two different schools in the same city, we kept in touch and met up from time to time over cups of coffee, glasses of beer, or some *tapas*. Jason was young and full of energy and happy to share his wild stories and misadventures. His tales of dating in Spain were hilarious and, while they seemed to always end in his rejection, they were punctuated by an optimism to continue meeting new people. He also took very easily to the *siesta* and didn't understand why it couldn't be adopted as a cultural practice back home in the United States. His spirits were high, and he had that special look in his eyes that said he never wanted to leave.

After a few months, however, his demeanor shifted. He was no longer euphoric. The Spanish women that rejected him became "inaccessible snobs" and he was sure the *siesta* was the cause for the economic woes the country was then experiencing. He started to stereotype the people of the country and their culture, seeing his experiences in Seville as emblematic of national archetypes—his complaints of a girlfriend named Soledad became issues of Spanish women in general. The issues and pessimism mounted and mounted, and after six short months he returned to the United States. Though I couldn't identify it back then, I now suspect that Jason was experiencing and succumbed to culture shock.

What is culture shock? Generally speaking, culture shock is a negative sensation or an anxiety caused by an immersion into a new culture. A popular analogy is that those who suffer from culture shock feel like a fish out of water.

They often report feeling alienated and detached. Culture shock is the experience where long-term travelers, when placed in new environments and new cultures, increasingly resent their host culture, become annoyed by it, and come to reject it as wholly or partially inferior to what they are accustomed to back home.

In some instances, the host culture might be radically different from what the traveler is accustomed to, like a New Yorker being immersed in the culture of rural Mongolia. In others, the new culture may share some commonalities, like an American immersed in British culture. The amount of culture shock an individual might feel can vary widely and depends as much on the person as it does on the environment. Put differently, an American living in England could experience a much more profound sense of culture shock than an American living in Mongolia. It really depends on the individual.

It is my experience that individuals who take part in long-term study abroad programs often experience culture shock, whereas short-term study abroad students rarely experience it. And this makes sense. A year studying in a foreign country is a significant amount of time to be immersed in a new world far from home. Conversely, short-term students may just decide to roll with the punches, knowing that their time is short. They may also deal less with the hassles and headaches of daily life, being that they have a tourist mindset and, well, a return ticket.

Not everyone who lives for an extended period of time in a foreign country experiences culture shock, but it is common enough for researchers to study it as a real phenomenon. Indeed, researchers have identified a common pattern among individuals who experience culture shock. Studies have found that there are a few phases or stages of culture shock.

They are:

1. Attraction
2. Annoyance
3. Adaptation and Adjustment
4. Acceptance

Researchers have also designed a U-shaped chart that symbolically illustrates the four-stage model of culture shock. It looks something like this:

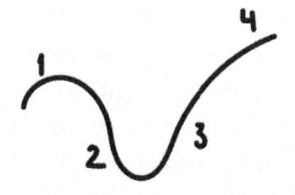

In the first phase, often called the "honeymoon" phase or the "attraction" phase, travelers are fascinated with the foreign land. Everything dazzles their senses, the food, the customs, the rhythm of life. They are highly motivated to see, do, and learn. They often report feelings of pleasure and confidence. However, at this stage, their level of interaction with the people and culture of a host country may be superficial. They may not know a lot about the culture they are visiting, their experiences being new and surface-deep. This is much like the experience of a temporary tourist, who proclaims, "I love it here! I can totally live here!" after a few fun days in a new city.

However, after spending a longer period of time in a new country, things begin to lose their luster, and the excitement of being in a new place dwindles. In the second stage, the "annoyance" stage, travelers often get irritated or express disparaging thoughts about the host culture. Generalities and stereotyping about the host culture often develop, and travelers begin to experience homesickness at this stage. They can often be heard making statements that claim their home country is superior to the host country. They often feel depressed, miss home, and do not engage with the host culture as much as before. This phase can begin anywhere from a few days to a few weeks to a few months after the "honeymoon" phase, depending on the individual.

If travelers can overcome the negativity and do not return home, the second stage will eventually pass, and they will begin to experience a new phase of "adaptation" or "adjustment" to the host culture. It takes some time to get to this stage, however, so they should not surrender during the difficult stage of annoyance and irritability. Conversations about the host culture begin to turn positive, and travelers look past the minor issues and prioritize the experience. Contentment begins to return, and travelers open up more but perhaps are still a little bit guarded, disparaging, or pessimistic.

Travelers will eventually adapt and feel at home in the host culture. They will enter the final phase of "acceptance" as they receive the host culture as their own. They feel at home and confident negotiating the host culture, and they accept the culture is as valid as their own culture. Nothing has changed in the host culture for the travelers to accept it; what has changed is their mindset. Unfortunately, this stage can take a long time to arrive at. It is often felt when travelers are confronted with the reality of their time abroad coming to a close or after they return home, where they experience difficulties reconnecting with old friends and family. This, by the way, is known as "reverse culture shock," the condition in which an individual no longer "feels at home" when returning to the country of origin. More about this in the last chapter of Part Four.

However, the older U-shaped graphical representation

PREPARATION, MINDSET, & INTENTIONS 63

of culture shock doesn't take into account of the growth that occurs by long-term travelers who overcome culture shock. It is as if all the difficulties, struggles, and revelations someone has during the process of overcoming culture shock are conceptually unimportant. I like to look at culture shock in a different way, one that takes into consideration the individual's growth, struggles, and development during the process. Here is another illustration of the stages of culture shock as a loop instead of a U-shape:

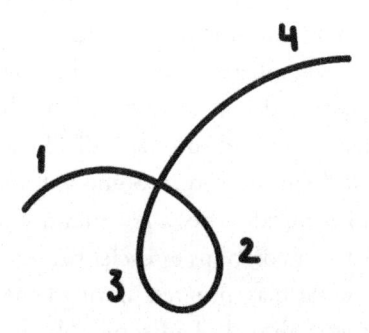

The loop model above, a diagram borrowed from Ray Dalio's book *Principles*, when applied to the stages of culture shock, takes into account the growth a long-term traveler will experience if the "annoyance" stage is reflected upon and worked on. In other words, if the travelers who are experiencing culture shock reflect and try to correct for the failures and difficulties they face, they may arrive at a better place.

Allow me to break down the loop model of culture shock further. In the first stage, the "honeymoon" or "attraction" phase, the individual is dazzled by the new culture and is in positive spirits. However, the individual may encounter some setbacks, difficulties, and annoyances. These hardships will continue and, hopefully, turn for the better in stage three when the individual begins to reflect and embark on a corrective course. Eventually, the individual will emerge from the experience in a better place. If and when an individual overcomes culture shock and arrives at the fourth stage of "acceptance," he or she has grown. The travelers who defeat culture shock may not be aware of it, but they will have grown and learned, catapulted to a higher state.

The point is that overcoming culture shock should be seen as a sign that the individual has grown in some capacity after a difficult bout. It means the individual has progressed beyond ethnocentrism, the idea that one's own culture and people are superior to another's. It means that the individual can see their home culture as one of many cultures around the globe, none being inherently superior or inferior to another.

There is some debate as to how long these phases last, but it ultimately depends on the individual. Some travelers may never feel culture shock. Some will progress through the cycle quite quickly, after a few months. Some may even go through a series of loops or cycles before eventually overcoming it. Some may progress through the cycle over the course of a year abroad. And some, like my buddy Jason, may never do so, returning home before they fully felt at home in the host culture.

I wasn't able to help Jason recognize that he was experiencing culture shock, because, as an international student myself, I didn't know what I was looking at. Just as a doctor doesn't know which disease to cure if he doesn't notice or understand the symptoms and their causes, study abroad students cannot overcome culture shock if they do not understand how it manifests itself. Knowing this information is empowering as you can self-diagnose, so to speak, your stage of affliction.

It may also be helpful to think of "culture shock" as "cultural adjustment" instead, something that every long-term traveler experiences in one capacity or another.

Embrace culture schock as a necessary step along the path of growth and development.

INTERCULTURAL SENSITIVITY AND INTERCULTURAL COMPETENCY

One night, when I was out eating dinner with friends in a quiet part of town, tucked away from the noisy and overpriced tourist areas of Seville, I met Charles. Tourists didn't typically visit that part of town, so when I heard a voice speaking English with an American accent, my attention was piqued, and I started a conversation with him.

Charles was an American student at the University of Seville. He was studying literature, so he was writing about his study abroad experiences on his blog. That night, Charles was writing a blog post about the lesser-known restaurants in town. We exchanged information, and the next day, I pulled up his blog. What I read appalled me.

To say that he was not enjoying his time abroad would be an understatement. His blog was mostly ranting, in which he found nothing but fault with his temporary home. To be sure, Charles was a good writer, which made his rants comical. And between rants were wonderfully written descriptions of neighborhoods and restaurants. But it was hard to see past the negativity.

For example, in one post, he discussed his frustrations at the closing of the stores during the *siesta* and on Sundays. He called the Spanish a lazy people who lacked a good work ethic. For Charles, the *siesta* was evidence to support his conclusions that they were culturally uninterested in economic advancement. For him, like Jason, it made sense that the Great Recession had hit the country so badly. Conversely, the United States, with its 24-hour Walmarts and uninterrupted 9:00 to 9:00 retail hours, was a far superior and rational model for a society interested in economic development.

It didn't stop there.

In another post, Charles criticized the nature of political engagement by the Spanish public, their protests and strikes amounting to little more than selfish inconveniences for everyone else. Elsewhere, he criticized Spanish food as being one dimensional, bland, and simple. He also spoke about how unfriendly the Spanish people were, especially when compared to the people in his hometown. He so consistently disparaged his host culture, finding fault with everything and anything, that I was surprised that he was not only still studying abroad but also sharing his rants with others so openly.

I get it. People need outlets. People need to vent their frustrations. But I viewed most of his blog as a cringeworthy exercise in viewing his own culture (which was my culture too) as morally, economically, and, in every other way, superior. Charles was clearly in the deep stages of culture shock.

But it might be too simplistic to claim his opinions to be merely symptoms of culture shock. That conclusion might prevent us from having a deeper conversation on the ways in which individuals deal with difference. And, it might prevent us from exploring the origins of culture shock and the conditions that amplify it. Researchers say that culture shock and its symptoms can appear when travelers aren't "interculturally competent" or "interculturally sensitive."

❧

Sensations of annoyance are common to the experience of culture shock. But culture shock could be seen as a symptom of a larger issue of intercultural sensitivity, which is a term used to describe the degree to which individuals experience cultural differences. That is to say, intercultural sensitivity attempts to measure how "open" or "closed" someone is toward foreign cultures in relation to his or her own culture. This sensitivity is related to intercultural competency, the skills and attitudes one develops and demonstrates when communicating, engaging, and sharing experiences with people from different cultures.

People can experience cultural differences, well, differently. And, as intercultural competencies are sets of learned skills, it takes time and effort to develop them. But, when done right and using some of the tips in this book, studying abroad helps develop your intercultural sensitivities and intercultural competencies.

The sociologist Milton Bennett developed a scale that illustrates the ways in which individuals deal with cultural differences. The scale, known as the Developmental Model of Intercultural Sensitivity (DMIS), helps us not only see that there is a range of ways people deal with cultural differences, but also that the ways in which we deal with cultural differences can evolve.

According to Bennett's research, there are two main ways in which travelers deal with the cultures they're experiencing. Bennett calls them the *ethnocentric* and *ethnorelative* stages. Generally speaking, in the ethnocentric stage, an individual prioritizes his or her culture over the culture they are visiting. Their home culture is not just the standard by which others are compared, but it becomes the "right" or "best" culture. In the ethnorelative stage, conversely, the individual does not prioritize his or her own culture and, instead, sees cultural differences as "relative."

HOW PEOPLE EXPERIENCE DIFFERENCE

ETHNOCENTRIC	ETHNORELATIVE
denial, defense, minimization	acceptance, adaptation, integration

Those in the ethnocentric stage deny that cultural differences exist, defend their own culture as superior, attack the culture of another, or minimize cultural difference, as they believe differences are minor. Those in the ethnorelative stage accept the idea that there are a variety of cultural differences, and therefore discussions, arguments, and statements of superiority are at best moot. They adjust their own behaviors while experiencing new cultures and eventually come to feel fully integrated in them.

Those who are expert travelers, ones who can negotiate cultures easily and feel at home in them, typically fall within the ethnorelative side of the continuum. Those who are in the beginning stages of culture shock or who are like Jason and Charles, often fall on the ethnocentric side of the continuum.

Some see this as a causality dilemma like "the chicken or the egg" problem. They question whether studying abroad opens students' minds, or whether students who already have open minds to begin with are the ones most likely to study abroad. It is probably a mixture of both.

It is important to remember that these are stages that you can progress through and improve upon. It is also important to remember that these are stages of evolution like the stages of culture shock. While Charles had some serious work to do in terms of developing his intercultural competency, he is not a lost cause. He can move from his closed-off, demeaning, and reactionary ethnocentrism into the more understanding world of enthnorelativism. And studying abroad gives him the opportunity to do so.

Take a moment to reflect on where you fit within Bennett's spectrum. How sensitive to cultural differences are you? Are you currently in the ethnorelative or ethnocentric stage? Do you think that cultural differences exist? Do you think one culture is inherently superior to another?

Understanding that there are different ways in which individuals deal with cultural differences, and that the experience of culture shock is one of the ways in which people deal with cultural difference, may give you the encouragement to deal with the symptoms of culture shock if and when they rear their ugly heads.

If you experience the symptoms of culture shock and ethnocentrism, try to embrace it as a necessary step along the path of growth and development. If you find yourself complaining a lot about the host culture you're visiting, feeling sensations of boredom, or wishing you were back home because you're "fed up" with the culture you're living in, then chances are you're in the middle of an important phase of growth.

As one scholar notes, "Once you realize that your trouble is due to your own lack of understanding of other people's cultural background and your own lack of the means of communication rather than the hostility of an alien environment, you also realize that you yourself can gain this understanding and these means of communication. And the sooner you do this, the sooner culture shock will disappear."

※

So, how does one develop intercultural competency? How does someone ensure culture shock doesn't win? Fortunately, there are some strategies to help individuals develop intercultural competencies that, as it turns out, will also help keep culture shock at bay. It just so happens that the ways in which one makes the most out of a study abroad experience are also great ways to develop cultural competency and help curb the negative sensations of culture shock. The strategies that will help defend against culture shock and will help ensure that you will make the most out of your experience

PREPARATION, MINDSET, & INTENTIONS

are detailed in Part Four, below. But, to give you a taste of what's to come, here are the main takeaways:

1. Staying healthy, both in body and in mind, is the foundation of a good experience abroad.
2. Avoid the temptation of getting distracted by social media and what's going on back home. Focus on the experience abroad.
3. Remember the reasons why you wanted to study abroad to begin with and achieve your goals.
4. Having friends from home is necessary, but focus your efforts on making as many foreign friends as you can.
5. Learn the local language.
6. Be open to new experiences, embrace the new culture, and get uncomfortable.
7. Become as familiar with your new home as possible.
8. Reflect on your experiences.

REFLECT

1. Have you ever spent time abroad and experienced culture shock? If so, what annoyed you? How did you deal with the annoyances?
2. Research the types of cultural differences you can come upon in the country you're studying in.
3. Prior to your study abroad program, write a few positive notes to yourself, seal them, and tuck them away in the back of a book or journal you're taking with you. Write about how happy, excited, and fortunate you are to go abroad. Write some encouraging quotes. If you experience culture shock abroad, open one and remind yourself how fortunate you are.
4. Ask yourself how open-minded you are about cultural differences. Place yourself somewhere on Bennett's spectrum, above.
5. Ask your friends and family to honestly rate you on how you deal with difference. Ask them to rate you on Bennett's spectrum and to give specific reasons for their ratings. Reflect on their answers. Are they right?
6. Could there be any cultural differences that are so objectively amoral that someone couldn't accept them? Or, should everything within a culture be considered relative?

9. IT'S TIME TO GO

It was a late October night, and I waited in line to order a pizza at a local restaurant. Immersed in writing my doctoral dissertation, I didn't have the time to cook. Trying to meet my writing deadline, I instead decided to pick up a pizza and, with greasy fingers, continue working, reading, and writing as I ate. Such is the life of a graduate student.

As I stood in line, a woman tapped me on the shoulder. "Excuse me," she said.

I turned around. She had a youthful expression, but from the white strands of hair at her temples it was clear that the woman had a few years on me.

"I'm sorry," she continued, perhaps sensing my confusion. "I just couldn't help but notice your shirt." I was wearing a thinning "study in Spain" T-shirt. "I majored in Spanish, and I actually planned on studying abroad in Spain. But," she said with a sorrowful smile, "life happened." Her smile was one of melancholy and regret.

"If you don't mind me asking, why didn't you study abroad?" I said.

"A boy. He didn't want me to go. And then I ended up following my—now my ex-husband—to another state after graduation. Things sometimes don't turn out as you expect them to."

Laments like these are not uncommon to hear. In fact, I hear them quite often. When I return from an international trip and hand students over to their parents at the airport, I'm met with gratitude for having taken their children abroad to have transformative experiences. They often reveal, however, that they wish they had done something similar when they were their children's ages. A tone of melancholy and regret is often heard in their voices.

Even someone as well-traveled as nomadic Matt Kepnes told me that he regretted not traveling earlier on a study abroad program.

If you follow the "Milton Bradley" path of life in America—high school, university, career, marriage, children, mortgages, retirement—you may never have the freedom, ease, or time to spend a considerable period in another country and get to know another culture in an intimate, meaningful way. If you are currently in university, or you are about to begin attending one, the time to start thinking about studying abroad is now. Conventional wisdom suggests that young adults and university students should explore the world before "life happens."

Many students wait until their junior or senior years to study abroad, and many of them—perhaps sensing that the well of opportunity has dried up for them—wish they would have studied abroad earlier as freshmen or sophomores.

I am of the opinion that you should study abroad as often and as long as you can. If you have the chance and financial resources to study abroad for a few years, you should take advantage of your good fortune and go for it. If you can only study abroad for one semester, go. Do whatever it takes and for however long. Just go.

It goes without saying that you can always travel when you graduate, when you are married, when you have kids, or when you retire. But now is the time in your life with the fewest number of responsibilities and demands on your time. Putting off plans of seeing the world until the future, which may never come and, therefore, isn't guaranteed, isn't smart thinking. And, as students often report, studying abroad can radically change the course of your life.

It did for me. And FOMO made it happen.

In case you're unfamiliar with the term, FOMO is an acronym for "fear of missing out," which refers to the anxiety

Conventional wisdom suggests that young adults and university students should explore the world before "life happens."

one feels when seeing other people (usually on social media) living their best, fun, exciting, and interesting lives. Sufferers of FOMO often feel depressed, isolated, and bored. They see their friends and acquaintances having amazing experiences, like riding camels in the desert, taking cooking classes with Italian grandmothers, and seeing ancient buildings, all of which they compare to their seemingly humdrum lives. In short, they are "living life" and having extraordinary experiences, and we feel terrible that we aren't doing the same. Research has shown that there is a correlation between social media consumption and depression.

But FOMO can be a good thing if it motivates you to study abroad.

It was, in fact, a motivating force for me to take the plunge and spend a year abroad. I had friends with lengthy international experiences, and they were younger than I was. They had lived in places like Korea, Mexico, and India, doing interesting things likes teaching English, participating in an artistic residency, and backpacking throughout the subcontinent.

I, on the other hand, only knew my own state with any degree of confidence and had only traveled with my parents on family holidays. The experiences my friends were having helped me reexamine my own life and made me question what I had been doing with it. In my defense, I was working on a master's and PhD. But I told myself as I was starting my doctoral dissertation, it would be now or never. FOMO took me by the hand and led me to study abroad.

Do not forget that the international experiences other people are having that you see on social media are within your grasp. You probably cannot afford the luxurious lifestyle that the "influencer" you follow on social media has. But going abroad, immersing yourself in new cultures, and seeing the world's wonders is within your grasp. You can either be a passive spectator to the experiences of others that show up on your social media feeds, silently cursing them while feeling miserable that your life isn't exciting, or you can be an active steward of your own life and cultivate similar experiences, adventures, and opportunities.

Studying abroad is within the realm of possibility, especially with the wealth of scholarships, grants, financial aid, and part-time jobs to help pay for it. Check the short section entitled "Money Matters" in the appendix of this book for more information on how to fund studying abroad.

※

Second only to not going at all, the most unfortunate mistake you can make is failing to take full advantage of your time abroad. I do not mean this solely in the carpe diem sense. I do not even mean this in the "study hard" sense. What I am referring to is neglecting to capitalize on your unique set of circumstances while in a foreign country.

Being in a new place will present you with a strange and unique set of experiences and opportunities that are wholly different from the country you just left. Think about the new sights, smells, sounds, and experiences that you do not have access to back home. Think about all the new opportunities you will have. This is what you need to focus on. And making the most of your unique set of experiences is exactly what the next few chapters deal with.

REFLECT

1. If you already know where you want to study, what unique set of circumstances do you expect to experience? Is it language, culture, museums, or access to professional opportunities? Do research and list them.
2. How will your unique set of circumstances abroad be different from what you're familiar with?
3. How can you take advantage of your unique opportunities abroad?
4. Can you think of any personal or professional goals related to your study abroad plans? List them.
5. If you don't know exactly where you want to study, then brainstorm some places that you're drawn to. Think about why you're drawn to those places, and think about how those places can help you with your academic, personal, and professional goals or help you grow as an individual.

Part Four
Study Abroad Missteps

"The encounter with the other is really, at its heart, an encounter with oneself. [. . .] Even in its subtler forms, the act of looking is an act of self-regard."

— Eliza Griswold

10. INTRODUCTION

As we have already seen, traveling can be defined as something more than the act of physical movement from one location to another. It can also be defined as the hard work, the struggle, and the internal growth associated with seeing the world. Thus, good travelers are often described as skilled individuals who move about gracefully, unfazed when confronting the inevitable delayed planes and screaming children, the missed connections and the downpours. They seamlessly integrate into the environment they visit as if they were locals.

Being a skilled traveler has just as much to do with having a proper mindset as it does with having experience with travel. This is to say that, traveling as we have defined it is a skill that you can learn. Unfortunately, it can be an expensive skill to acquire as the practice requires the act of traveling.

Travelers unskilled in the art of travel often commit a variety of blunders, some of which include expecting that everyone speaks English, not trying to speak the local language, not being sensitive or cognizant of the local culture or traditions, unabashedly ignoring local laws and customs, and pretending that all civilized and social rules of decorum, like speaking softly in places of worship and waiting in line, all but disappear while traveling abroad. I've actually seen a tourist elbow his way to the front of a crowd to view a painting instead of waiting in line and, in a final act of insolence, snapped a quick selfie with it before elbowing his way back through the crowd.

Without a doubt, studying abroad puts you at risk of committing the same mistakes as any other traveler. However, given the length of time you will be abroad, more will be expected of you. Outlined in the chapters that follow are, in my opinion, some of the most egregious social, cultural, and travel blunders to avoid while studying abroad or traveling for an extended period of time. By avoiding these mistakes, you will have a more fulfilling experience and your worldview will transform into one that is cosmopolitan in nature.

Cosmopolitanism has little to do with mere worldliness or being able to navigate diverse cultures. It is something far deeper, one that the clinical psychologist Theodore McEvoy describes as "a more profound and inner development."

Few would dispute that travel can help a person understand, tolerate, and respect different cultures and ways of living, that it can provide the traveler with new and diverse points of view. Travel gives you the opportunity to consider notions of cultural relativity and, therefore, reflect on whether or not it is okay to judge one culture with the ideas and standards of another.

Travel is not just about the "other," it is also about the self. It encourages self-reflection about one's place in the world, hopefully removed from or cultural bigotry or patriotic zeal. Dr. McEvoy calls this "self-objectivity," or the ability to see oneself and one's place in the world more objectively, more rationally, and more internationally. It is to look at yourself and your culture in the mirror, so to speak, honestly and in a critical way. Travel gives us this gift.

Studying abroad and international travel also give the individual the ability to view and understand the world and its history more deeply. They help the individual cut through the noise of modern life and focus on what is important and timeless. They provide an opportunity to the traveler to see historical and cultural depth instead of the superficial dazzling or charming phenomena of a place. If you are studying abroad, you have the ability to cultivate these inner transformations. Dr. McEvoy acknowledges that the seeds of such transformations "are especially apparent in those youths who have most successfully encountered and mastered sustained cross-cultural experiences."

Part Four of this book will help you identify the common missteps study abroad students make, and give you the tools to help you avoid them and thus grow as an individual and world citizen. They will help you have a more successful, enriching, and rewarding study abroad experience. Along with stories of experiences abroad, I will describe behaviors to avoid and behaviors and actions to cultivate.

Travel can help a person understand, tolerate, and respect different cultures and ways of living, that it can provide the traveler with new and diverse points of view.

11. NEGLECTING HEALTH

It happens every year. I get off an airplane with twenty sleep-deprived students and force them on what I like to call the "march of death." We drag our bags across town and check into the hostel where, in a move that elicits heavy sighs and curses, we forgo resting and immediately go on an introductory walking tour of the city. With my coleader and the tour director at the front of the pack, I usually walk toward the back of the group to prod along sleepy-eyed stragglers. The day is designed to be intense, not simply because I can finally gloat over my resilience when compared to the twenty-somethings but also to help them overcome jet lag and get into the rhythm of being in a new time zone. As you can imagine, they get cranky. They pretend to be more upset at the fact that their feet and shins ache than being kept awake unnaturally, a lie they can no longer tell when they pass out at the table during our welcome dinner.

I'm sure most people would suffer like my students if forced to walk as much as they did, with as little sleep as they had. But the fact that they're American makes the experience more difficult for them. American students are, generally speaking, not as accustomed to walking as much as their European counterparts. A recent study concluded that the average American walks under 4,800 steps per day, which comes to around 2 miles (3.2 km) a day. This puts the United States behind countries like France, Germany, Spain, the United Kingdom, and Russia. While the study also correlates this data with other factors, like a city's "walkability" and the built environment, the numbers are interesting to think about.

Chances are that if you are from the United States and are studying abroad, you will regularly have days where you will walk more than you've walked all week back home. You will likely be in a dense urban environment and without a vehicle. You will likely walk to class, walk to the grocery store, walk to the bank, and, well, walk everywhere. Many students actually enjoy walking everywhere, not just because it means they're free from vehicles and their costs but also because it helps keep their bodies active.

Generally speaking, individuals who walk more on a daily basis are healthier when compared to those who walk less. But resist the urge to necessarily equate an increase of walking with an increase of healthfulness. The simple act of walking is good, but it does not necessarily result in self-care. As you can imagine, there are Europeans in poor health who walk five times as much as Americans each day. Moreover, as the number of steps increases, so does your caloric demand. And many Americans—already accustomed to larger portions—might find themselves indulging even more after a long day of walking.

While it doesn't take much for students to think about questions of health and physical fitness during international programs—indeed, something as simple as an increase in walking could do so—it is surprising to learn that nearly 25 percent of study abroad participants in a survey reported a negative change in their physical health, perhaps due to being in a new environment with a new diet, lifestyle, and habits. Interestingly, only 11 percent of participants reported a positive change in their physical health. This means nearly 66 percent of students reported their physical health staying the same and not changing for the better or for the worse. This is surprising considering the overwhelming consensus in the medical and scientific communities that something so fundamental to the human experience as walking can have real health benefits.

What does it mean that nearly 66 percent of students report no change? Does it suggest that a majority of study abroad participants continue their habits while abroad? Do study abroad students walk just as little as they did back home? Or, are the health benefits simply imperceptible after a semester or year? These questions remain unanswered. What is not ambiguous, however, is the fact that a quarter of all study abroad students report a negative change in their health and wellbeing, more than twice the percentage of students who reported a positive change.

The report did not explain why or how students' reported health had changed. Do students consider their time abroad to be temporary and, therefore, indulge in food and drink more than they would otherwise? Do they perceive themselves as being on holiday or on vacation, falling prey to unhealthy foods, habits, and behaviors?

While traveling, it is easy to let yourself go, so to speak, using the excuse "I'm on holiday" for indulging in food and drink, you must remember that studying abroad is not a vacation. Studying abroad doesn't give you a pass to develop bad habits or to neglect your health. Remember, travel requires work and effort, stressing the body and the mind, so it does not make sense to neglect your physical and mental health while putting increased strain on them.

※

I wasn't strong enough. I had tried and failed. And now I found myself walking into a café around the corner from my apartment in Seville and sliding coins into the vending machine. Out slid a pack of cigarettes.

I had smoked cigarettes in high school and during my early college years, but I had kicked the habit just before starting my master's. I began rock climbing and running and felt I was in the best shape of my life. Moving to Spain proved challenging, however. In Florida, smoking in public places like restaurants had been outlawed since the early 2000s. There was also a successful moral campaign against smoking in the United States. In Spain, however, smoking in restaurants and bars was still permitted under the law. Smoking also didn't have the same sense of moral outrage in Spain as it did in the United States. It seemed everyone smoked in Spain, and the very first sensation I had in Spain was seeing and smelling the clouds of cigarette smoke hanging in the terminal of Barajas Airport.

Desperate to assimilate into Spanish culture, I found myself smoking again. I stopped exercising, grew out my beard, and started hand-rolling my cigarettes. Who had I become in a few short months? Spanish hipster.

Fortunately, midway into my time in Spain, I was able to slap myself awake. I began running along the Guadalquivir River and through the backstreets of Triana. I also began climbing again, this time under the various bridges of Seville. My health was improving.

But I discovered that, in addition to helping my body and mind, exercise helped me learn my surroundings more intimately and helped me cultivate more local experiences. It also helped me make more local friends. During my morning runs throughout my neighborhood, I discovered hidden nooks and courtyards, hole-in-the-wall restaurants and bakeries, and other interesting places well off the beaten tourist path. I also met a small rock-climbing community that climbed under a few of the city's bridges, who took me on their monthly climbing trips deep into the Spanish countryside. I would not have experienced any of that had I not decided to pay attention to my health.

One of the lessons that I learned was that, while the specifics of my immediate surroundings had radically changed, I should have considered my study abroad experience as an extension of my experience back home. I enjoyed running and rock climbing back home, and I should have continued the practice abroad from the outset. I had quit smoking cigarettes, so I should have resisted the urge and temptation to light up again. Instead, my health and lifestyle had dramatically changed in only a few short months. It is easy to fall behind.

HOW TO STAY HEALTHY WHILE STUDYING ABROAD

It goes without saying that staying healthy is important, regardless of where in the world you might be. Fortunately, staying active abroad is quite simple. Below are some tips to help you stay healthy abroad.

Continue your exercise routine abroad. If you enjoy running, playing sports, practicing yoga, going to the gym, meditating, or doing anything else active back at home, continue the practice while you're abroad. It also has the side effect of helping you make more friends and having more meaningful experiences. If you do not exercise back home, doing so abroad is as good a time as any to start.

Drink in moderation. Undoubtedly, you and your friends will have drinks in bars and party in nightclubs. That's great! I'd be disappointed in you if you didn't have fun on that level. But being moderate in your alcohol consumption helps avoid negative health consequences and social and safety risks. Please see the Appendix for more information about staying safe.

Make your own food. As it is with alcohol consumption, moderation is key with your eating habits. Eating at home not only helps you save money but also helps you keep tabs on what you put in your body.

Cultivate the right mindset. Staying healthy also depends on having the right frame of mind. Avoid the "but I'm on vacation" excuse for eating poorly and neglecting healthy habits while you're studying abroad. Understand that your study abroad program is an extension of your education and normal life, just in another country.

Don't neglect your mental health. Homesickness, culture shock, and situational depression are common within the study abroad community. If you're studying abroad with an American program, your program may have counselors and mental health resources. Check with your program. Also, review the section above that deals with culture shock so you can identify the symptoms. Luckily, some believe that engaging with the culture in which you're living, having meaningful experiences, and making local friends help stave off depression related to studying abroad.

Have a tribe. While in the next few chapters I will recommend that you cultivate more local friends than friends from your home culture, having a tribe of culturally similar friends is helpful, especially when the study abroad blues strike.

A NOTE ON HEALTH INSURANCE

I would be remiss if I didn't touch upon health insurance. This topic has been covered by others elsewhere and at great length. But, to be brief, there is a good chance that if you are participating in a long-term study abroad program with an American institution, your school will provide you with some type of international health insurance policy. If you're not being provided health insurance, I highly recommend that you purchase coverage on your own. Traveler's health insurance is not as expensive as health insurance in the United States, fortunately, and you may be thankful for the small price you'll pay.

If your program is offering an insurance plan, you'll likely have an orientation session that details the procedures to use it should the need arise. Please, please, please do not skip the orientation session that deals with the insurance policies and procedures. Have a large cup of coffee before the session, ask questions, and take notes. Know this information very well. Take thirty minutes out of your day to wrap your head around your policy. You don't want to be in the difficult place of trying to understanding medical and insurance terminology in another language while also dealing with the pain of a broken bone.

Traveler's health insurance is a great business, as a large majority of travelers return from their adventures without injury. Chances are, you will too; but it is important to not let the statistics give you a false sense of confidence that it can't happen to you.

If you take medication, be sure to talk with your doctor about how to deal with medication abroad. If you're in a short-term program, you will likely need to bring with you the necessary amount of medication. If you're in a long-term program, ask your doctor about your options to obtain your medications abroad.

REFLECT

1. What will you do to keep your mind and body healthy while abroad?
2. If you enjoy playing team sports, what are the opportunities to participate in them while you are abroad?
3. What are some situations and temptations that you should avoid in order to remain physically and mentally healthy?
4. Do you have any health-related concerns? What can you do to avoid aggravating them?
5. Does the study abroad program you're participating in offer health insurance? If not, research some traveler's health insurance companies, weigh the pros and cons of each, and purchase the coverage that works best for you before going abroad.

12. GETTING DISTRACTED

Gregarious, respectful, and funny, Nicholas was well-liked by the other students on one of my study abroad programs to Europe. He was well-liked by the professors too; his essays, wonderfully written and thorough, were always of the highest caliber. Nicholas had never been out of the country and was a positive influence in not just getting the class excited but also by forming bonds and relationships with his classmates in the weeks before travel.

In the study abroad programs I lead each year, I ask students to write their term papers on works of art and architecture that they will see during the program. So, that year in Italy, a sense of pride washed over me when I saw the group of students excited to encounter the works of art they had been studying—spending quality time with the art, taking notes, and listening attentively to the guides when they spoke. That is, the entire group of students except for Nicholas.

Nicholas was one of the worst-behaved out of the group when abroad. It was not that he broke local laws. It wasn't that he was a mean and terrible human being either. It was that Nicholas got distracted in the worst possible way. He wasn't distracted by artistic beauty or dazzled by a new place. Rather, he was distracted by his smartphone.

Nicholas, having a data plan on his phone, often wandered away from the guide to take and post selfies on social media, often enlisting the help of other students to help take photos for him. This didn't stop even after the gentle reminder to the group to be respectful and to pay attention to the guide. The behavior continued despite the reminder that the students needed to pay attention to produce the required academic work.

When we visited Nicholas's term paper topic, St. Peter's Cathedral, I had hope that visiting the church would be the moment when Nicholas started to pay attention. Here, I thought, Nicholas would stand near the *baldacchino* and see the rays of light flood the church and have a revelation that to engage with the place he was visiting was the whole point of the program. I was wrong. The jokes and distractions continued, and I observed him showing an American music video on his smartphone to the other students.

I get it. Expecting someone to be 100 percent focused and engaged in this era of smartphone distractions might be a bit much, especially so for millennials. But this was his term paper's topic. This was his research. This was his class. This was his grade. This was his time in a new country. Is it too much to expect a student who voluntarily signed up for this study abroad program and this term paper topic to actually give a damn?

Needless to say, the research paper that Nicholas produced was the worst that year. It was bland, full of historical errors and banalities, and lacked depth, detail, and insight. In fact, his research paper was a mere account of what he saw as a tourist instead of the meaningful analysis we had been preparing them to write. What happened to Nicholas? How could he have transformed so quickly from a model student with potential into a dud? It wasn't that he was unprepared. Just the opposite. The rough drafts he produced were excellent.

It seems like he wasn't distracted by the right things. Instead of getting "distracted" by the new world he was experiencing abroad, he was distracted by his smartphone and the culture of his home.

The story of Nicholas is not unique. It illustrates a phenomenon of distraction that plagues travelers and study abroad students alike. It is one thing for travelers to get captivated by the new culture they are visiting. This is kind of the point of travel. And, arguably, this is not "distraction." It is the opposite: "awareness." It is quite another thing, however, for travelers to get distracted by the culture from which they come, which pulls them back home and glues them to the world they were supposed to leave behind. It pulls them away from the present moment, the uniqueness of the place they've visiting.

A survey given to study abroad students a number of years ago asked them to indicate all perceived academic or personal changes, either positive or negative, since arriving overseas. This study revealed the two highest-reported negative changes were study habits and an ability to concentrate. A large 41.6 percent of students reported that their study habits worsened and 40.7 percent of students reported that their ability to concentrate decreased. Four of the next six highest-reported negative changes related to reading. Some 38 percent of students stated they read fewer newspapers, 32 percent reported reading fewer magazines, 25 percent said they read fewer works of fiction, and 21 percent revealed that they read fewer assigned texts.

On one hand, these are alarming statistics. After all, the individuals surveyed were students who participated in study abroad programs. If the point is to *study* abroad, why are students reporting their study habits, reading habits, and concentration on the decline?

On the other hand, these statistics make a lot of sense. After all, students are in a new environment with a plenitude of distractions. Who has time to read newspapers, periodicals, and novels, especially if it is more difficult to find those materials in the English language while abroad? And who wants to sit down in a room with a book when there is an exciting new city outside?

I wish Nicholas would have been more distracted by the new place he was visiting and less so by his smartphone.

It is okay to be "distracted" by your new environment. The point of studying abroad is to absorb as much of the new culture as possible. So, if learning about a new culture momentarily takes you away from learning about whatever is in your textbook, that may not be so bad. As I mentioned earlier, paying attention to the new world that you inhabit, getting "distracted" by the new sights, sounds, textures, and tastes is not, in fact, distraction at all. Rather, it is awareness and focus and a central objective of the study abroad experience.

HOW TO STAY ENGAGED ABROAD AND NOT GET DISTRACTED

It is fashionable nowadays to evoke mindfulness and meditation as a way to focus and stabilize the mind, to protect it against the nonstop chatter of the mind, to ground the self. Albeit trendy, there are some interesting and applicable ideas related to mindfulness that can help with distraction while abroad.

One such idea is a concept called *shoshin*, which comes from the Japanese Zen Buddhism tradition and means something like "beginner's mind." It is a concept that can be referred to as being in a childlike state of wonder, having an open mind, being curious, and willing to learn.

Leaving your phone at home or simply powering it down is another way to help you not get distracted. Doing this will help you avoid the automated behavior of picking it up to check notifications. Think about it. How often do you instinctively pick up your phone, open an app, and scroll through a social-media feed without really being focused or aware as to what you are doing? More importantly, if you're not even aware of what you're doing in virtual reality, how could you possible be aware of what is going on in actual reality?

Walking meditations are also helpful in getting to know your place. As you walk throughout your new town or city, focus your attention on sounds, both near and far. If you catch your mind wandering, bring your attention back to hearing whatever sounds arise in the external world. You can also pay attention to sights and people instead of sounds, trying to be aware of what it is you're seeing. Try to take notice of what you sense in the present moment. Techniques like these may help you "pay attention" to a place in new ways.

You could also take a micro-adventure to a new place alone. Taking a day trip to a new nearby town, village, or park without the distractions of a companion or a smartphone will give you the time and space to experience someplace in a mindful way.

REFLECT

1. How often do you instinctively reach for your phone and flip through social media? Try to catch yourself doing this and keep a tally on how often this occurs.
2. If you suspect you have a problem with social media or your smartphone, consult a screen-time app to see how much time you're actually wasting.
3. When you're abroad, experiment with leaving your apartment without your smartphone. If you're resisting this idea, what is holding you back? What do you think you'll miss by leaving your phone at home?
4. Leave your phone behind and go on a walking meditation for one hour in your new city, focusing on the unique sounds. If you get distracted in thought, bring your attention back to the sounds. What did you learn?

Being dazzled by the new world that you inhabit, getting "distracted" by the new sights, sounds, textures, and tastes is not, in fact, distraction at all. Rather, it is awareness and a central objective of the study abroad experience.

13. FORGETTING WHY YOU'RE THERE

It was a Wednesday night, and I was packing my bag for a short visit to Madrid. Waiting for me in Madrid was the Royal Academy of History, a three-hundred-year-old institution with an extensive historical archive. As the archives I needed to access were in Madrid, living in Seville proved to be challenging.

Fortunately, the director at the school I worked in was friendly, and she allowed me to work from Monday to Wednesday, which freed up the rest of the week for me to research and write and work in the archives in Madrid. This arrangement was ideal. I could take the overnight bus from Seville and head straight to the archives after arriving in Madrid. It was not always comfortable, but I needed to make it work if I wanted to finish my dissertation.

My apartment was in Triana, a quiet neighborhood in Seville and just a short walk from the Guadalquivir River. Near the apartment and along the river, however, ran a street called Calle Betis, which came alive at night with crowds of students drinking and dancing. My friends had planned on meeting up for a drink on Calle Betis that Wednesday night, and the moment my phone buzzed I knew why they were texting.

"Meet on Betis in 30," the message read.

"Maybe. Madrid tomorrow," I replied. I tossed my phone on my bed, finished packing, and glanced at my watch. It was 9:00 p.m.

My phone buzzed again. "Just one drink."

I walked out onto my terrace. The evening sky was a deep blue, and the weather had a crisp note to it for the first time that fall. High in the sky, I heard a steady wind blowing, which occasionally came down and whipped through the streets below. Illuminated in golden light, the spires of nearby churches and the Giralda appeared over the red tiled roofs of the neighborhood. I pulled the fresh air into my lungs and responded to my friend. "Okay. Just one."

Thirty minutes later I was walking down the street toward Calle Betis, where I quickly found my friends making a great deal of noise. In their hands, tall and skinny glasses of what was likely rum and cokes.

My happy friends greeted me with strong American hugs and two Spanish kisses. Soon, I found myself holding my own rum and coke. *Just one drink*, I thought as I looked at my watch. It was nearly 10:00 p.m.

You know how this story will end. One drink led to two. Two to three. And somewhere between three and four, I stopped checking my watch. The next time I glanced at my watch was when one of the nearby bars began shuttering its doors. I had missed my bus.

"You can always go another time," my friend said to me.

There was nothing I could do at that point to catch my bus to Madrid. That ship had sailed. *Tomorrow*, I thought. I'd wake at a decent time and catch an early bus to Madrid. Sure, I'd lose a half day of work in the archives, but I could always make it up by going back to Madrid the following weekend.

The next day, my alarm clock rattled me awake and I slogged through the headache to catch the morning bus to Madrid. I slept the entire way, awakening only upon arrival in Madrid. I went to the archives and tried to work. My head was foggy, and I had the taste of rum in my mouth. After a few pointless and unproductive hours of scanning texts and mindlessly copying documents, I gave up and told myself that Friday would be more productive.

But the temptations continued.

"Are we still on for dinner? Meet at 9 okay?" my friend texted me. I had forgotten that I made plans with one of my friends who lived in Madrid. Being that I was eager to meet more local people, I consented. And surely another drink or two—the metaphorical "hair of the dog"—would help me feel better.

The night turned into another bruiser. I met my friend in the Mercado San Miguel, drinking wine and vermouth and eating tapas before heading out for a few beers and pizza at a restaurant called Mastropiero in the Malasaña neighborhood. Afterward, we found ourselves playing pool, drinking beer, and dancing in iconic bars like La Via Lactea. I looked down at my watch: 4:00 a.m.

"I have to go. Archive work tomorrow," I said abruptly. I made my rounds saying hasty good-byes and stumbled my way back to my hotel, which took another thirty minutes by foot.

I did not even make it to the archive the next day. My research trip to Madrid was a complete bust. I had wasted my time and money. I felt ashamed for several weeks. Sure, I'd had fun with my friends. Sure, I'd had a (somewhat) memorable night.

But, in large part, the fleeting experience of drinking with friends had taken precedence over the very reason for me moving to Spain: my research. I felt like a fraud, like someone who had poor impulse control, like someone behaving frivolously who could not stand up to these types of pressures. In short, I was ashamed and defeated.

But in my defeat, it dawned on me that playing pool in smoky bars, dancing the night away in discotheques, and drinking too much did not provide any new experiences in and of themselves. While the superficial phenomena of the experience was new—being in that particular place, in that particular time, with those particular people, sounds, and smells—the more general experiences of going to bars, drinking, eating pizza, and playing pool were not unique.

After all, there were bars with pool tables back home. There were plenty of nightclubs back home, which played the same songs. There was plenty of alcohol and beer back home. In other words, I wasn't really doing anything new. Rather, I was doing everything old. I was merely taking part in what anyone could do almost anywhere else on the planet. I probably would have felt less guilty having missed the archives for a cultural experience that I could not replicate back home.

I came down hard on myself not just for having fun. I am by no means a puritan when it comes to having a good time. Instead, I came down hard on myself for having fun at the expense of my work and for being irresponsible.

Don't get me wrong. Blowing off steam is often necessary. However, there is a problem if having fun gets in the way of the entire point of your being abroad to begin with.

But, I was conflicted. I didn't want to travel to Spain and not enjoy myself. I didn't want to spend every last second of my time in an old archive writing and reading. I didn't want to say no to experiencing Spanish culture firsthand. I didn't want to say no to enjoying myself from time to time. So, I decided that I wouldn't shun my friends or stop socializing with them, but I would act in a more responsible way when it came down to working toward my goals. I decided that I would work hard and play hard but eliminate the latter if it compromised the former.

HOW TO STAY PRODUCTIVE ABROAD

You will likely have a different situation than I had. I only had a few days each week in which I could do my academic work. You, on the other hand, will have a different experience if you are in a long-term study abroad program. You will have classes to attend. You will probably have cultural excursions planned for you. You will have plenty of time to get your work done, without the need to travel halfway across the country. But the principles of staying productive are universal.

Planning is essential in the study abroad environment. Consider all the distractions you will be presented with in your new home away from home. Think about all the temptations. Planning is critical.

And planning is essentially time management. And it is not a difficult thing to do. What you want to do is schedule your time abroad so that you can steadily achieve your goals. You don't need to be so rigid that you're scheduling your lunches and pee breaks. But if you plan out your goals, you will likely have a better chance to realize them.

Remember your SMART goals from earlier? These are the goals that you should consider when thinking about time management and planning. You will have a regular course schedule if you are studying abroad, so plan your goals around your course schedule.

Take advantage of your smartphone's calendar app or go old school and buy a day planner. Consider scheduling an hour's worth of studying immediately after each class. I know studying after class is not cool, especially when your classmates invite you to grab lunch with them during that time, but you will likely be in a better place academically by doing so. And, the best part about sticking to your schedule is that you won't feel guilty when you are out having fun.

Generally speaking, packing too much in is never a good idea, especially when it relates to suitcases, mouths, and studying. Cramming does not really work in terms of memory or skill development. So, do not pack all your homework into a Sunday evening. You may not have the time to complete it all, and if you do, you may not be able to remember anything after the class. It is best to spread your work and learning over a period of days. Spreading work across several days gives the brain a period of rest, and helps you approach the work from a fresh perspective. If you are writing a paper, for example, spreading the work over several days gives the writing some space to grow and develop.

This is not just about studying. This is also about learning new skills. The individual who practices an instrument a little bit every day in a week progresses more quickly than the individual who practices the instrument for a long time once a week. Cognitive scientists agree with this conclusion and refer to this as the "spacing effect." Simply put, cramming is not an effective way to learn.

Unfortunately, I cannot give you a template of a schedule. You will likely have a customized course schedule, and I don't know what time of the day you are the most productive or what your habits are. You should probably figure out when you're the most productive, and schedule your most critical goals during that time. Consider scheduling your minor goals, or less cognitively strenuous ones, during times when you typically do not have a lot of productive power.

DON'T BREAK THE CHAIN

Along with planning, forming habits will help you achieve your goals. One method to cultivate habits to achieve goals is called "don't break the chain," which comes from Jerry Seinfeld. If we are to believe the story, a young comedian once asked Jerry Seinfeld if he had any advice on being a successful comic. Seinfeld told him that he must write better jokes, and writing better jokes involves writing jokes every day. Seinfeld advised him to purchase a large wall calendar, to hang it where he could see it, and to put a large red "x" through each day he worked at his goal of writing jokes. Working each day at a goal will create a series of red x's on the calendar, thereby creating something reminiscent of a chain. Keeping the calendar conspicuous will shame you into accountability, reminding you not to "break the chain."

So, if your top goal is to be fluent in Arabic, and one of the ways you will achieve that goal is to study vocabulary, then you must schedule time to practice Arabic vocabulary each day for, say, thirty minutes. Every day you study thirty minutes will earn you a red x on your calendar. The goal is to have a calendar full of red x's.

This is an easy way to visualize at the end of the week or month how much effort you spent in pursuit of your goals. If, at the end of the month you only have 5 red x's, someone could legitimately ask how committed you are to achieving your goal. By not breaking the chain, you ensure that you work consistently toward your goal and are set up for success.

If buying a wall calendar is too old-fashioned for you, there are some useful (and free) apps that help you keep track of your habits. Simply search for "habit tracker" in your smartphone's app store to find them. These work in the same way as "don't break the chain." In the app, you list the goals you want to work on and mark the days when you work on them. They are convenient, as you can track a series of habits in one place to visualize how often you work toward multiple goals. This is also helpful to keep track of your CHASE experiences.

You can also keep track of your habits through bullet journaling. Simply search for "bullet journaling habits" to learn more, or for more information visit:

https://studyabroadinstitute.org/students/habits

REFLECT

1. Self-assess your willpower and fortitude for resisting the urge to be unproductive. Do you typically have a problem with achieving your goals? Do you easily surrender to peer pressure and abandon your work?
2. What are the temptations you currently cannot resist?
3. Which of the techniques above do you feel comfortable using to ensure that you work at your goals every day?
4. What are you usually doing when you find yourself distracted? Surfing the web? Playing on your phone? Hanging out with friends? Watching television? What can you do to minimize those distractions?
5. What distractions and temptations do you envision you will face while abroad? What do you think you will be able to do to keep yourself from succumbing to these distractions and temptations?
6. What does your current study schedule look like? What times of the day are you most productive studying, reading, and writing for academic purposes? Do you pack everything in on the weekends? Or, do you distribute the workload throughout the week?
7. When abroad, commit to having a set study schedule.

14. NOT MAKING LOCAL FRIENDS

Toward the end of my second semester living in Spain, I met up with Samantha again. She had a few hours to burn in Seville before meeting her family, who were arriving later that day.

It had been a while since she and I last saw each other at the *auxiliar* meet-and-greet, and I was interested in seeing how her experience was turning out. How was she getting on? Had she figured out what she wanted to do with her life? Was she having a good time? These questions, however, were answered as soon as the waiter came by the table and asked us if we wanted another drink.

"What did he say?" Samantha asked, turning to me puzzled.

The waiter held his thumb to his mouth. "Would you like another beer?" the waiter said in English, his accent thick and his tone impatient.

"Ah. Si. Un otro mas," she replied, clumsily. The waiter nodded and left with our empty glasses. "I still can't understand them."

We laughed it off, but I was perplexed. Samantha had been in Spain for two entire semesters, living in a small pueblo in the mountains, yet she still didn't have a command of the language enough to understand a simple phrase from a waiter. To be fair, language learners often find the accent in southern Spain to be more difficult than the accent from Madrid or Latin America. And she was teaching English after all, which required her to speak English all day at work. But she only worked part time, which meant she had many opportunities to speak Spanish if she wanted to. So, everyday questions and conversations, such as "Would you like another beer?" that have the body language and situational contexts to help, should have been easy.

"You've been here for nearly eight months!" I said, laughing. "Why can't you understand them?"

The excuses came. Their accent was too thick. It was not as proper as the Spanish she'd learned in school.

But languages can be learned, and accents are always relative to the accent that someone learns first. So, I came to the conclusion that the problem wasn't necessarily the language or the accent. Rather, the problem was something deceptively simple.

"Do you have any Spanish friends?" I asked. "An *intercambio* maybe? Work friends?"

"Well," she said, pausing to grab the glass of beer from the waiter. "It is hard to make friends here. But I *do* have friends. They are the girls I moved here with."

※

Without a doubt, making friends away from home can be difficult, especially when the culture you are living in is different from your own. It can be difficult due to the wide array of cultural rules for forming and maintaining friendships, which vary from culture to culture.

Making new friends at home can be hard enough. But it can be much harder to make friends when you're adding new languages, social cues, and traditions that you're not totally familiar or comfortable with into the mix.

For study abroad participants and long-term travelers, it is important to strike up a balance in your social network between new foreign friends and friends belonging to the cultural group you belong to. Sure, it is easier to communicate with and relate to peers from your own culture, but relying on them too much could rob you of one of the most important and rewarding aspects of the international experience: making foreign friends.

It should be obvious why it is important to make personal connections with the locals while abroad. But if it isn't, let me explain. Making foreign friends abroad helps you better and more easily understand others and their values and biases. And it helps you more clearly understand your own values and biases. It helps you more easily and more successfully interact with and relate to people from other cultures. And, most important of all, it helps you develop a more nuanced and a more sophisticated understanding of the world.

Imagine all the potential friendships and experiences that Samantha missed over the course of two semesters because she did not try hard enough to make more Spanish friends. After all, locals know all the secrets to their community that tourists overlook. They know the best places to go to, the most interesting things to do, and the best restaurants to eat in. Locals are the potential keys to "authentic" experiences abroad.

I am not here suggesting that you should avoid being friends with anyone from your home country. Quite the opposite.

It is essential to have a group of friends from a similar culture, as their camaraderie is unmatched in dealing with stress reduction, homesickness, and low morale. Friends from your home culture more easily understand you, and feeling understood is valuable. So, don't forgo making friends with someone from your home culture. Rather, aim to have a healthy balance of foreign friends and friends from your home country.

HOW TO MAKE FOREIGN FRIENDS

Think back to your high school or middle school days. Did a foreign exchange student ever stay with you or someone you knew? Did you become instantaneously curious about the new person? Did you talk to them and take the time to befriend them? Have you ever experienced the painful chore of repeating phrases over and over, ever more slowly, so that they or anyone else learning your language could understand what you were saying? Have you ever patiently waited for a nonnative speaker of English to form basic sentences in their thick accents? Whether or not you've had experiences like these does not matter. What matters is understanding that you may become the exchange student in the scenarios above. You will be the one with the thick accent. You will be the one struggling to communicate. And you will be the one having a hard time befriending others because of it.

Making friends can be a difficult endeavor. Making friends with foreigners can be even more difficult. Not only does language sometimes get in the way of forming relationships, so do cultural differences. Generally speaking, the more quickly you learn the cultural codes of the country you will be studying in and the more quickly you learn the language, the more quickly you will be able to make friends. However, if you have yet to master their language and culture, you can still make friends with the locals. It happens all the time.

Many people simply will not care to be your friends. People often already have their social groups formed by the time they reach university, and breaking into a preexisting group is difficult. But that is okay, because out of every fifty people who do not care to engage with a foreigner or care to have new friends, there will be one or two who do. The people who are willing to give you the time of day are the people you need to cultivate friendships with. Whether they are young or old, funny or serious, handsome or ugly, consider accepting any individual showing a genuine interest in becoming friends.

You may be asking, "How do I make friends if I struggle with the language?" Consider putting yourself out there. What I mean by this is that you should talk to as many people as possible. Chat up the baker, the store clerk, the bartender. Smile at them. Ask them questions. If they are one of the few who are curious, a conversation will naturally occur.

You are not going to befriend everyone, but the more people you chat with, the more opportunities to form friendships you will have. Don't expect people to go out of their way to start conversations with you, so you will need to take responsibility here.

Truth be told, it is easy to meet new people and make new friends in nightclubs and bars. I mean, that's kind of the point of going to them, right? Get a few wingmen and head out to the club. Chat with people. Take numbers and hand yours out. Who knows? Maybe you will make a local friend. While I think regularly patronizing nightclubs with your hometown friends while in a foreign country is somewhat counterintuitive to the point of studying abroad, there is a time and place for it, especially if it involves an opportunity to befriend locals.

Another strategy for making friends abroad is to look for other foreigners, but from different countries. One of my closest friends in Spain was a Sicilian student named Alessandro. We were from distinct cultures, but we experiencing similar circumstances and became friends. Together we met many people, including a group of French students who, like the American students we knew, clustered together and only spoke to each other in French. But by befriending the French students while I was in Spain, I was able to learn about the broader European culture. As a bonus, I learned a little French while doing so and, more importantly, met my future wife.

Other strategies to make friends include enrolling in recreational sports leagues, taking cultural classes like those for song and dance, volunteer for organizations that you support, and look for opportunities to network and socialize with new groups of people. Talk to as many people as possible in areas and on topics that interest you.

TRAVELING WITH FRIENDS

It was the summer of 2009. A swine flu epidemic had been rocking Mexico and was the topic *du jour* on all of the news outlets. The virus infected tens of thousands of people, killing hundreds, and Americans began to worry that the flu would spread from Mexico and into the United States.

Perhaps foolishly, but also knowing that Mexican tourism had been suffering, I thought that it was a good time to travel to Mexico. The main issue that I encountered, however, was that none of my friends were interested in going with me. If it wasn't the flu my reluctant friends were concerned with, it was surely the drug cartels' violence that peppered the same news reports.

All my friends made it clear that, if I wanted to travel to Mexico, I'd be going alone. So, in June of 2009, I found myself standing alone on the curb outside of the Miguel Hidalgo y Costilla Airport with a forty-liter backpack on my shoulders and a return ticket home in two weeks.

It turns out, though I was scared shitless on several occasions (have you ever been ordered to place your hands against the side of a bus and get frisked by a group of plainclothed commandos with assault rifles?), it was one of the best decisions I ever made. I traveled from Guadalajara to Zacatecas to Guanajuato to San Miguel de Allende to Mexico City at my own pace and without any real plan. I made friends on that trip with whom I still communicate. I felt, for the very first time in my life, that I was free and was experiencing something that I had cultivated on my own.

Sure, I had been to Mexico before. But that was in a prisonlike resort with my parents when I was ten. We strolled up and down the carefully manicured beaches of the resorts and ate all we could at the all-inclusive resort restaurants. This time was different. I walked up and down the dusty streets of the cities and ate fruit cups and tacos from curbside cooks. On our first trip, people that looked like our neighbors back home surrounded us in the calm waters of the Caribbean. Now, strangers of all stripes surrounded me in the central markets and squares.

It was during the summer of 2009 that I, unwittingly, first got a taste of the sweet pleasures of solo travel. I learned a lot about myself on my first solo trip to Mexico, which also helped me cultivate a spirit and love for adventure. I also learned a lot about another history and another culture, much of which—I suspect—would have been lost on me had I followed the paths, interests, or schedules of a companion.

It may seem paradoxical, but one of the best ways to make local and global friends is to travel alone. Solo travelers get lonely, and the loneliness forces interactions with others. You will talk to far more people if you are alone, and far more people will talk to you. Resist the thought that solo travel means antisocial travel. It is anything but. Also, while solo travel comes with a certain set of unique risks, it isn't inherently risky. See the appendix for tips on staying safe abroad.

Students often plan to study abroad with friends in the same destinations. I understand why. Life is more enjoyable with friends. But the argument can be made that studying abroad with friends limits an individual's growth and learning abroad. Friends who often study abroad together rely on one another too much, cling to one another too much, and miss out on many of the opportunities to speak with new people in new languages about new things.

Lamentably, I've seen students drop out of their study abroad programs when they learned that their friends could no longer go. Several students were on the waitlist of a program I was leading to Europe. We had one spot open on the program, so we sorted the applications by strength and offered the available spot to the top applicant. She, however, asked if there were two spots open and if her friend could also go. Her friend was also on the waitlist, but she was much further down on the list. We reiterated that there was only one available spot and asked her again if she wanted to claim it. Then came the unexpected. She asked if she could give her spot to her friend, as it was her friend who had the original idea of studying abroad to begin with. Neither of the students participated in the study abroad program that year.

Hanging out solely with people from your home culture while you are studying abroad is just as problematic as bringing a friend along with you. And chances are you will have plenty of opportunities to fall into that trap. As I mentioned earlier, many large universities in the United States have international centers where students from the same university study. For example, my alma mater, Florida State University, has study abroad centers in Florence, London, Panama, and Valencia. There, cohorts of students enrolled in the university travel abroad together and continue their studies. While an individual in one of these programs may not plan on studying abroad with any friends, they will be placed in an environment surrounded by other students from their hometown, home state, or home country.

While these university programs are often great, I find them inferior to programs that sit students alongside foreign students. Placing twenty-five lonely American students in the same room in a foreign country will result in those students becoming friends at the expense of them doing the challenging work of forging foreign friendships.

Again, one of the main points of studying abroad is to immerse oneself in a new culture. Hanging out with a group of friends from the same state does not sound like an immersive international experience to me. In fact, it can be quite costly to the experience.

As I mentioned earlier, university study centers can also be quite costly in another way. They are expensive, often costing as much as $13,000 or more per semester. Why then would anyone pay thousands of dollars to immerse oneself in another culture only to be limited in terms of how much of that other culture one is really immersed in?

The point is not to bash university study centers in foreign countries; they provide great opportunity, experience, and value to students.

The larger point is that the lonelier you are, and the more you separate yourself from your own culture, the better positioned you will be to have global friends and experiences.

To be sure, it is more challenging to travel to a foreign university alone. It is intimidating to uproot your life and leave behind your friends to go study in a foreign country without a support system. But, if we are honest with ourselves, we know that this is the entire point of studying abroad. If you want to hang out with your friends in another country, you can always plan a holiday with them.

Making friends is hard—especially in a culture with which you are unfamiliar—but with high risk comes high reward. Had Samantha decided to travel to Spain without her friends from the United States, she may have had more local friends and spoken better Spanish. And speaking foreign languages just so happens to be the subject of the next chapter.

REFLECT

1. Do you have any foreign friends? What is great about them? In other words, what are the virtues and rewards of having foreign friends? What are some difficulties?
2. What do you do in your spare time? Write down a list of your hobbies and free time activities. Feel free to flip back to view your SMART goals, as there might be some overlap. These present potential opportunities for meeting new people.
3. If you already know where you will be studying abroad, begin searching online for activity groups related to your hobbies. Search through websites like Meetup.com to find people and groups with similar interests.
4. Leverage social media. Find people who are doing the things you enjoy doing in the city you will be studying in. For example, if you are interested in poetry, use social media to search for and connect with people and groups who organize open mic nights or literary events. Put yourself out there.
5. Search for interest groups and tours like food crawls and tours in your host city. Popular hostels are typically reputable sources of information about them. Sure, these cater to tourists, but foodie tours put participants in a social mood and setting while teaching much about the local urban environment and culture.
6. Will you study abroad with friends from your home culture? If so, what could you do to ensure that you will try to make local friendships and connections? Do your friends share the same desire and drive to make foreign friendships? Do you and your friends share a hobby like soccer, something that you could do together with a larger group of local people?

7. Do you make friends easily? When was the last time you made a new friend? How did you do it? Did you initiate the friendship or did the other person? Write down some of the ways you remember being the person who first initiated new friendships.

"Travel is a state of mind. It has nothing to do with existence or the exotic. It is almost entirely an inner experience."
— Paul Theroux, *Fresh Air Fiend*

15. NOT LEARNING THE LANGUAGE

Samantha's tale is one that reminds us how cultivating local friendships and learning local languages are intimately connected. Simply put, she was not able to capitalize on an opportunity to advance her linguistic development, because she did not cultivate many Spanish relationships, platonic or otherwise. If done right, a student immersed in Spanish culture for a year would, at the very least, be able to order another a drink at a restaurant. But before we judge Samantha, understand that this misstep is extremely common.

An old friend of mine married and moved to Holland with a European woman he had met during his travels. She spoke a few languages, including English, so they could communicate without problems. One day, about three years into his stay in Holland, my friend and I Skyped. As we shared stories about the difficulty of living abroad, the subject of friends came up.

"Do you have a lot of friends?" I asked.

"Not really," he said.

"Why not?"

"The friends we have are mainly my wife's friends. It is hard to make friends here."

"How is your Dutch?"

"Not very good," he admitted. "I don't have the chance to practice. Everyone here speaks English as well as I do. I can get by without it."

I remember thinking, *What a shame. How can someone live in a country for so long and not learn the language? Why on earth hasn't he tried harder? Can't he at least sign up for language classes? Wouldn't he absorb some by simply going about his daily business?*

Learning a new language is a difficult and intimidating task. It is downright hard. But there is no better place to learn a new language than in its country of origin. It is not that my friend wasn't intelligent. He was. His problem was—like Samantha's—probably a mix of shyness, intimidation, and laziness.

Making mistakes in a language you're learning—especially basic mistakes—can be embarrassing. Nobody likes to be laughed at for saying something incorrectly or unintentionally humiliating or offensive. We all are afraid of being misunderstood, of mispronouncing simple words, and of not making any sense at all.

Get over it. Upon hearing you speak, any native speaker will immediately understand you are a foreigner and, therefore, overlook your mistakes. You are learning the language, after all, and mistakes are necessary components of language acquisition. Think about, for example, a child speaking, making mistakes, and inventing words; the parent understands what the child means and corrects her. Eventually the child learns. As nobody mocks or admonishes the child who is learning a new language, nobody will mock or admonish you for your mistakes as you learn a new language. Only jerks would ever mock or admonish anyone for this. And who cares what jerks think anyway?

If you are not strong in the language you want to learn, it is easy to keep silent. However, keeping silent is the best way to remain weak in the language. Spoken-language fluency is more difficult than being able to read a language or understanding the language being spoken. Being able to speak requires a set of skills that can only be acquired by speaking. So, wrestle with the language. It is in your failures that you will grow. Understand that you will make mistakes. Understand that you will have an accent. Get over it and start speaking.

Learning a new language is as difficult as it is time consuming. It takes a significant amount of brainpower to process information on the fly, to recall the correct vocabulary and conjugations, to articulate something coherent. It takes time to learn how to speak because of the vocabulary and memory required to say the right thing in the right way.

The larger problem that plagues many Anglophone travelers is that they don't try hard enough, that they don't care to learn another language, as it is "unnecessary in this day and age to speak a language other than English." Visiting any beach town on the southern coast of Spain or on the eastern tip of the Yucatan Peninsula will present to you a world of British and American English-speakers who refuse to speak anything else because, like my friend in Holland, they believe "you can get by without it." This smacks of arrogance. But they have a point.

English speakers have it good at the moment. English is the world's *lingua franca*. The term literally means "Frankish language," a reference to an historical language adopted by the early modern Mediterranean world to facilitate trade and communication among people who had different mother tongues. There have been several of these so-called "bridge languages" throughout history, such as French and Latin. Today, English is probably the most spoken of these bridge languages. And one does not have to look far to find examples of this in action. Among my circle of friends in Florida, the native languages of some of the couples are Swedish and Spanish, Portuguese and Russian, Spanish and Polish, and English and French. What language do we all communicate in? English.

Technically there are more native speakers of other languages, like Chinese and Spanish, in the world, but there are more people around the world who learn English as their second language. Get off the plane in Marrakech or Bangkok, Mexico or Bali, and you'll find local English speakers eager to chat you up in English to earn your trust and, of course, your tourist dollars.

Adding to the argument that learning another language is unnecessary are these little supercomputers that we all keep in our pockets. It is all too easy to call up dictionaries, verb conjugators, and real-time translators on our smartphones to help with our communication. Why, then, would any English speaker need to study and struggle with learning another language when everyone else already speaks English, and if not, anyone can quickly open an app and get a translation?

Those points are hard to argue against from a utilitarian or practical standpoint. But the multitude of benefits—including social, neural, and cognitive benefits—of learning a new language is clear.

Learning a new language gives you entry into a world you wouldn't otherwise have access to by relying on smartphones or other people to speak your language. Venture outside of the tourist areas and major metropolitan zones and the number of English speakers drops off radically. You cannot rely on English speakers if there are none around. At that point, smartphones and apps become important if there is signal. But relying on smartphones for communication limits someone's ability to penetrate, understand, and participate in another culture. How deeply can someone really enjoy another culture if they rely solely on an app?

A veritable world of social opportunities and experiences opens to those who speak local languages, so much more than to those who do not. People who try to learn a new language also experience similar opportunities. You get invited to events and dinners. You are able to have conversations with more people about more things. You can form relationships with more people and on a deeper level, making more friends and connections.

In addition to the social and cultural benefits, learning new languages also has brain-related benefits. Studies show that learning languages helps combat age-related neurological decline. It also helps individuals learn better, have better memories, and be more creative.

If that weren't enough, there are also career-related benefits. Most people whose mother tongue is English cannot speak another language. According to one recent study, about 80 percent of all Americans cannot speak a second language. Learning another language, then, puts you in a small minority of individuals who can communicate with a wider group of individuals more effectively, thereby giving you an advantage in your life or career.

HOW TO LEARN LANGUAGES WHILE STUDYING ABROAD

Let's be real. You are not going to master a foreign language during your ten-day study abroad program. You may not even master a foreign language on a year-long program. But it should be obvious that an individual who is exposed to a language for an extended period of time and who puts in the effort to learn the language will emerge from an international program with better linguistic skills. There is no excuse to spend a semester abroad in a foreign country and not at least try to improve your foreign-language proficiency. In other words, if you travel abroad on a semester-long program to Italy and you don't emerge with a basic understanding of Italian, you've done something wrong. You must do whatever you can to learn the language, lest your in-country experience remains superficial and your time be wasted.

The city in which you will live is an immersive language classroom. It is, in fact, the best place to practice. You can literally test your abilities at any second and around any corner. You can get immediate feedback from local speakers. If they do not understand you, you will know that something is wrong. If you say something incorrectly, someone will likely correct you. Think of the foreign city as one large language lab, in which its inhabitants are unwitting language teachers. The multitude of mundane experiences gives you opportunities to advance your foreign language skills.

But that is not enough. While helpful, language practice in everyday situations only goes so far in developing your language acquisition. You must seek out meaningful connections and attempt to engage in conversations that are above your level. Your approach to learning the language should be one that is deep and wide, not superficial and narrow. Cast a wide net, taking advantage of all the resources you have available.

If you plan on studying abroad in a place where you do not speak the language, then it is essential that you make learning the language a top priority. If you are strong in the language but not completely fluent, this is your opportunity to step up your game. The following tips will help you learn a new language while you're studying abroad.

- Find a language-exchange partner or, better, make locals your core group of friends.
- Take formal language classes.
- Watch the local television stations.
- Read the local newspapers.
- Watch foreign movies with English subtitles.
- Watch a documentary or read the news in the local language on a topic you already know a lot about.
- Reread a book you've read, but in the target language.
- Strike up conversations with strangers at the store, on the street, or at a bar.
- Ask someone for directions, or if someone looks lost, ask them if they need help finding their way.

- Join social, artistic, and/or sport groups.
- Attend a few social events each week.

You will not absorb a language to a level of fluency just by living in another country. Likewise, do not assume that just because you're studying abroad that you will inevitably interact with native speakers outside of the classroom environment. You must make an effort to interact and learn the language. One study recommends the following strategy to make the most of international experiences in order to advance in a foreign language:

- Learn about the nature of your study abroad program in your host country, and have realistic expectations about your linguistic development. The beginner should not expect to become fluent after one semester abroad.
- Understand that some of your classmates will be foreigners like you, so do not spend all your time with them if you wish to learn the local language.
- Strive to develop meaningful connections, communications, and interactions with native speakers.
- Make goals and push yourself out of your linguistic comfort zone.
- Reflect on, journal about, and attempt to improve upon your situations and shortcomings.

Another study found that students made significant gains in second-language acquisition with preprogram preparation in the target language. For example, students who take several semesters of Spanish prior to traveling to a Spanish-speaking country emerge from their study abroad programs with a better level of Spanish than students traveling to a Spanish-speaking country without the predeparture training. A little goes a long way.

Interestingly, the same study found that students who spoke with their home-country classmates in the target language did not improve their skills as much as students who didn't speak with their classmates in the language. This last point suggests that talking to a friend with whom you share a common culture in the foreign language that you both are trying to learn is hazardous to your foreign-language development and proficiency. In short, it is better to practice your new language with locals who have native proficiency than with your friends with whom you're studying abroad.

REFLECT

1. If you know your study abroad destination, self-assess your language ability. You can find basic proficiency tests online. What is your level? Where do you want to be when you're done with your program?
2. If you are an absolute beginner, what can you do beforehand to start working on your language skills? If your level is intermediate, what can you do to master the language? If your level is advanced, what are your areas of weakness, and what can you do to improve upon them?
3. When it comes to learning a new language, what are your fears or weaknesses? Think about what you can do to overcome them.

4. Prior to travel, download a foreign language app to your smartphone or computer and practice each day. Regular intervals of practice, even if twenty or thirty minutes per day, have a compounding effect and will help your language-learning pursuits.
5. How can making foreign friends help you increase your foreign language proficiency?

"To walk down a street is an immediate, irrecusable experience for which no hypothesis about a city, however ingenious, can be a substitute or as instructive."

— Simone de Beauvoir, *The Long March*

16. NOT GETTING UNCOMFORTABLE

The waiter dropped a small tray of white fish onto the table. The peculiar mix of smells—fish, vinegar, and garlic—was first stamped on me then. I looked at my new friend Jorge suspiciously.

"The *boquerones* are the best here," he said in Spanish.

"They look interesting," I said as I poked at one with a toothpick.

"What, man? Have you never tried them?"

"No."

"Why not try one first? Judge later."

I pierced one of the small, white fillets with my toothpick and brought the limp carcass close to my face. I examined its slimy texture.

I never appreciated seafood as a child. My seafood experience was limited to crustaceans, and I avoided consuming all other forms of marine life. Growing up, I lived in a beans-and-rice, steak-and-potato household. We reserved shrimp and crab only for special events. Fish never appeared on our plates.

Jorge stabbed a garlic-and-vinegar-infused slither and slurped it into his mouth. He smiled, smacked his lips with delight, and washed down the slimy treat with a sip of cold beer. "Nothing is better than *boquerones* and Cruzcampo on a hot day," he said smiling.

"What the heck," I said and I slurped the cold, garlicy fillet down.

A world of pleasures had suddenly been revealed to me. In a gastronomic experience that paralleled a religious awakening, it was love at first taste: I had fallen in love with *boquerones en vinagre*, and every time I return to Seville, I make it a point to meet up with Jorge at our favorite *boquerones* restaurant.

This experience was radically different from one I had recently leading a study abroad group of twenty-somethings to Spain. It was a large group, and we had arranged a tapas crawl through Granada. The idea was to expose the students to the region's traditional specialties and some of its newer gastronomic innovations. We had split the students into two groups and began our tapas crawl. What I had expected to be a culinary eye-opener for our students was actually a mouth-closer. Some of the students were hesitant to try new foods. Their hesitation was not simply because of dietary restrictions, as we made special accommodations for those students. Rather, some of the students refused to try the food because they prejudged that it would be bad.

From the perspective of a program leader, the tapas crawl was a low point for me. I felt as if I had not communicated well enough to my students that these types of experiences were the entire point of studying abroad. And, to be honest, sending back plates of specially prepared and untouched food was embarrassing. I later found out that some of the students visited an American fast food chain that evening. The point of studying abroad was lost on some of the more finicky students that night.

I am not trying to wag my finger and sound holier-than-thou about travel. But if the point of studying abroad is to experience new things, to expand one's mind and expose it to new ideas and cultures, then some of my students failed the assignment that night. As McEvoy notes, "the American student in Madrid or Bordeaux whose world is that of a little America might just as well stay at home. There is no intercultural exchange." To be sure, it is possible that you will learn that you, in fact, do not like a particular unfamiliar food. But when that happens, you learn something. And that is the point.

Of course, the previous examples are somewhat basic. But they cut to the heart of what travel is all about: seeing new things, experiencing new cultures, meeting different people, getting uncomfortable, and growing. Sticking to what is comfortable goes against the purpose and the benefits of the entire study abroad experience. I am not recommending that you take risks that will put yourself in harm's way. Nor am I recommending that you take risks and do things that will go against your religious or moral tenets. But one must get uncomfortable in some capacity.

Students and other long-term travelers must have open minds while visiting new places—whether concerning food, politics, or anything else. I am not saying that you must enjoy, accept, or adopt everything different or foreign. The point is to try to be receptive to new ideas, sights, and sounds. To be accepting does not mean to "agree with." To be accepting merely means to accept the fact that other people live differently than you. I do not eat whale or dolphin meat, and I think there are ethical concerns in doing so, but being accepting acknowledges that other people in other cultures do eat those types of meat and have no ethical concerns doing so.

Being accepting also does not mean that you cannot be an active participant in the exchange of ideas. Remember, studying abroad is about cultural exchange. As such, it does not prevent you from conversation and discourse. As McEvoy tells us, cultural relativity is "the capacity for understanding the cultural values and mores of other peoples, and a respect for and tolerance of their values and mores—specially those that differ from one's own. It is, furthermore, the capacity for questioning critically and objectively, in a constructive and instructive manner, the values and institutions held inalienable or sacred in one's own social milieu."

Thus, being "open" while studying abroad

- increases the extent to which we take part in intercultural exchange.
- helps us have new experiences.
- demonstrates and teaches trustworthiness and receptivity to new ideas and experiences.
- teaches us to avoid prejudgment.

We all think we are open-minded, receptive to new ideas and experiences. Studying abroad will test this assumption and, if you come to realize that you do not have an open mind, it will help you crack it open.

REFLECT

1. Make a list of five things that you can do in your destination city that you cannot do at home.
2. Make a list of the local foods in your destination city that you do not eat at home and that sound unappealing to you. Could you be persuaded to try any one of them?
3. What risks can you take abroad that will help broaden your horizons without compromising your health, safety, or personal beliefs?

17. NOT CULTIVATING A SENSE OF PLACE

It was 3:00 a.m. and the cold rain had finally slowed down after an entire day of deluge. The rain, in fact, convinced me to stay at the party longer than I originally planned, so I took the chance to walk halfway across town—drained after a long night of socializing—as soon as the rain took a more gentle turn. Unsure if the rain would pick up again, I was zipping through the small streets of the Macarena, in and out of those charming alleys and one-way streets beloved by visitors to Seville, when a voice called out to me.

"Pardon me," a woman said in Spanish.

Startled and weary, I turned in the direction of the voice and saw a group of shadowy figures standing before me.

"Yes?" I answered, keeping my distance and tapping my umbrella on the wet cobblestone.

"We're a bit lost. Can you help?"

I took a few steps closer and saw three middle-aged women huddled together. One held a map. Another squinted at a street sign.

Judging them not to be a threat, especially since I was the one who looked like I was up to no good—a swarthy man with a long beard walking alone through the streets of Seville in the middle of the rainy night—I approached the group.

"Where are you going?" I asked.

"Triana," one woman said.

I turned to the woman holding the map. She held it in the wrong direction.

"For some reason," I said, "many of the tourist maps of the city are oriented with east facing upward." I helped the woman turn it in the right direction.

"But, these streets are labyrinthine," I said in Spanish, casually dropping a recently-learned word, "and, in fact, Triana is where I am going. You can walk with me there if you want."

They agreed and I led them like Virgil into the dark, shadowy unknown. In hindsight, I wonder how they felt that night as a stranger led them down the narrow, dark, and lonely streets of the city, ones that took sudden and obscure turns. I wonder how they felt with my constant reassurances. "This way is quicker." *This is what kidnappers or serial killers say when they are luring their prey*, they must have thought.

Eventually, the bridge connecting Triana to Seville emerged before us, indicating to them that I was not a psychopath and that their destination was just on the other side. This must have reassured them, as their sudden chattiness demonstrated. But one woman then said something I will never forget.

"Your city is beautiful."

My city? I had been in Seville for about eight months by that time. *What do you mean "my city"?*

"Indeed," I said, "I wasn't sure about it when I first visited, but now, I admit, I love it."

"You're not from here?"

"No," I said, feeling a little smug. It was a small victory that they didn't detect my accent, never mind the fact that they really hadn't talked to me very much anyway.

"I'm from the United States."

"You don't say?" the woman replied. "I couldn't hear your accent, but now that you mention it . . ."

Damn it!

"Anyway," the woman continued, "you know this city very well. The streets are too confusing. We've visited Seville several times, but we get lost every time we come."

"I suppose the streets are easy to learn when one walks down them every day," I offered before parting ways.

I had not thought about Seville being my city until the stranger mentioned it. All I had done was promise to not let the medieval, haphazard streets of Seville confuse me. I was determined to know the city well, as if it were my own, to know it like the back of my hand. I knew this would happen by spending not only a great deal of time understanding the map but also many hours walking the city.

I had made mental points of reference. That's the street where so-and-so lives. That's the orange tree I climbed on a dare. That's that alley that leads to my favorite restaurant. By going out and experiencing life in the streets, I was able to transform the unknown space of Seville into a known place full of experiences, meaning, memories, and future nostalgias.

This idea first came to me as I was studying Yi-Fu Tuan's *Space and Place: The Perspective of Experience*. One of the underlying ideas throughout his work is that a place is a space that has meaning. A "space" is an unknown expanse. Spaces might be ambiguous in the mind—indistinct and unclear, somewhere devoid of meaning, an abstract notion. It is a space, perhaps, of discomfort or of danger, the unknown.

However, once an individual explores a space and imbues it with meaning, it transforms into a "place." The streets, locations, and zones begin to take shape and have meaning through experiencing them. A place is comfortable, safe, and known. A place gives an individual the satisfaction of feeling like "being home," perhaps an experience of a "home away from home," a feeling of comfort that only comes with knowing a place well.

In studying abroad, you have a special opportunity to transform a vague, far-off, and unknown space into a place, one full of meaning, memories, and experiences. This is your chance to know a strange city well, as if it were your own home, and develop the memories and sentimental attachments that you will carry with you for the rest of your life.

I didn't know that the attention I gave to my city, to wandering its streets, to getting lost, to exploring its nooks and crannies, of being curious and keeping my mind open to new experiences and meeting new people, would make me feel, when I revisited the city a few years later, like I was returning home. There still was something comfortable and familiar about the place, its smells, people, sounds, and sights. Turning around a corner would reveal before me forgotten memories of this or that day with so-and-so. There is a satisfying feeling of "being home" that comes with familiarity with your temporary home. And this comfort will create the wonderful feeling that you are returning home when you revisit years after your study abroad program.

There is also something quite satisfying about the idea that there is a city somewhere in the world that has a special place in your heart, a city that you will never forget, one that you will forever dream and reminisce about, one that stirs your memory and imagination, and one that makes you nostalgic for times past.

You cannot cultivate a sense of familiarity with a city you do not spend time getting to know. The burden is on you to make your new home familiar. Refusing to engage with and explore a new city or town will do much to prevent you from considering it a special place.

※

An American acquaintance of mine lived in nearby Malaga, an old city situated in southern Spain and on the Mediterranean. As a large city, Malaga has an international airport that gives opportunities for sun-starved European travelers to visit Spain and for wanderlustful Spaniards to visit the rest of Europe. My friend in Malaga acted more like the Spanish and seemed to always be visiting new places.

Following him on social media was an exercise in envy. He took classes from Monday to Thursday, after which he hopped on the budget airline Ryan Air to other European cities for absurdly low costs. Each week, it seemed, he posted pictures from a far-flung city.

He's living the life, I thought. Here was this young man, who hasn't even finished his BA, with the opportunity and financial resources to travel around the world. *He has been to more countries and has seen more cities in the last semester than I have in the last thirty years!*

Early that summer, before he returned home from his semester studying abroad, I asked him if I could crash on his couch; I had an early morning flight to Lisbon from Malaga, and he'd save me at least twenty euros and possibly from suffering bedbug bites at a local hostel. I'd even buy him a beer or two for his kindness. He agreed.

He was extremely friendly and welcoming, a good host even, but our conversations about the city made it seem like his knowledge of his city was like mine, as if he were a tourist with a short layover in the city.

I did travel around Europe, but not nearly as often as he. I did see new cities and countries, but not nearly as many as he. While he experienced a certain breadth and cultivated a sense of space, I experienced depth and cultivated a sense of place. In hindsight, I have no regrets that he and I did not share a similar experience.

It is understandable that when studying abroad you will want to take advantage of your new geographic region and use it as a springboard to explore other countries. For instance, Rome will surely tempt you to take trains to the other Italian cities or to hop on budget airliners to explore other cities in Europe. This is to be expected and highly recommended! Why not take advantage of that opportunity?

Some students studying abroad see their opportunity to live abroad as a "gateway" to explore the rest of the world. While the student experiences a breadth of experiences and cultures around the world, they may not experience cultural depth associated with knowing a place intimately well. Thus, students often get greedy for visiting new places, often preoccupied with the act of checking cities off their bucket lists to merely say that they've been to X countries before they reached the age of Y, as if that number alone is a trophy in and of itself.

To the person who crows about visiting all fifty states and thirty-five countries before the age of thirty, I respond, "So what?" This illustrates nothing, except, perhaps, having financial means and time. Boasts like these are akin to someone saying that they have read only a paragraph out of each book on a bookshelf, understanding very little about each one's plot, characters, and nuances.

HOW TO TRANSFORM A SPACE INTO A PLACE

How do you turn a study abroad space into a place? You must inhabit it. You must be intimately aware of it. You must make and cultivate experiences within it. Transforming a space into a place is about spending time somewhere just as much as it is about building relationships and friendships there. In fact, the two go hand in hand, for the wealth and quality of your experiences in the city will multiply when adding a little companionship.

Another way to ensure that you can cultivate a sense of place is by being familiar with how public transportation, if your city has any, works. Understanding the local bus, metro, and train networks is a mark of knowing a place well, actually using them, a mark of integration. Some cities have resident passes that offer discounts for frequent use, which you should absolutely consider purchasing if you plan on using the public transport system on a regular basis.

Studying a map will help you gain a sense of place. Get a physical map of your city and pin it to your bedroom wall. Most importantly, cultivate experiences by making a habit of exploring areas of your city off the tourist trail.

TIPS

1. Do you already know which city you will be living in? If so buy a map of the city and pin it to your wall. Do not rely on your smartphone's map. Get a large printed map. Try to understand your adoptive home conceptually and mark points of interest. If you are already abroad, get a free tourist map from a nearby hostel—or purchase a more detailed one from a tourist store—and pin it to your wall.
2. If you are walking across a city with your friends, try to be the leader. By "leader" I mean the one who has looked at the map in advance and already knows the way.
3. Do not rely too much on your smartphone's map when abroad. Try to memorize the directions to a place, only looking at your map if you lose your way.
4. Identify whether or not your study abroad destination has a "tourist core." If it does have one, and most large cities do, identify its boundaries on a map. This will help you identify the nontourist areas to explore.
5. Consider writing a blog about your city's restaurants, shops, venues, plazas, and attractions. Or, write reviews on sites likes Yelp and Google. This will help you create meaning and memories.

6. What interesting attractions or cities can you visit that aren't too far from your city? Go on day trips to explore them using public transport.
7. Research small local festivals in neighborhoods or in nearby towns, and visit them with friends.
8. Do you feel that you have a terrible sense of direction? What can you do to get better? Consider orienting yourself by making mental markers out of local landmarks. Start slow, but explore farther and farther, gradually.

18. NOT REFLECTING ON THE EXPERIENCE

Our caravan had just passed through a small oasis. Palms and little tufts of vegetation grew out of the clay-colored sand. I was expecting the view to open up into the vast and flat expanse of the Sahara Desert beyond the oasis, but large dunes obscured the horizon. When we came upon our camp, it was surrounded by mountains of sand, as if it were a village in an arid alpine valley or on the planet of Tatooine. At nightfall, a fire supplied us with two of the rarest commodities in the desert at night, light and heat, around which we gathered to enjoy conversation.

A few friends and I were in Morocco, where we hired local guides to take us into the vast unknown. While one of the guides spoke English, the other did not. But we all tried to communicate, in their bad English and in our bad French. Conversations often move beyond the banal when you get a chance to spend a few days with strangers in a place like a desert. One such conversation turned personal.

"Do you have a wife or a girlfriend?" one of the guides asked me.

"No," I said. "Single. What about you?"

"No wife. Not yet. But I have someone in mind. Near Marrakech."

He took out his mobile phone and showed me an image of a young woman. The mobile phone was not particularly "smart," its small screen limited to the top half of the clamshell design. But, despite the poor resolution, I could make out a young woman with a beautiful smile.

"She's pretty," I said. "How long have you two been together?"

"Not long," he said looking down at the phone. "We are not—what is the word you use?—'dating.' I like her. I think she likes me. I will try to marry her."

"Does she know your plans?

"Yes. I bought her a mobile phone."

"What?" I said, snickering. "You bought her a phone? And now she knows you want to marry her?"

He pulled his eyes off his phone and looked at me. He wasn't laughing.

Shit. I just laughed in this guy's face during a vulnerable conversation, and I'm in the middle of the desert with him.

"Sorry," I said. "I didn't mean to laugh at you. It's just that I've never heard of someone giving a mobile phone to a love interest. Things are done differently where I'm from."

Apologizing helped. He wasn't insulted or offended, thankfully, brushing off the confrontation as a cultural misunderstanding and taking the time to explain how his approach was atypical and modern—his words—in the culture of courtship among Berbers in Morocco.

※

I had traveled to many countries by that time, seeing real poverty and the beautiful resiliency of people in their struggle for comfortable lives. This visit, however, was my first trip to a predominantly Muslim country, not to mention my first time in Africa. The typical clichés of exoticism—the new sounds, colors, and fragrances of the space—charmed me like a snake. This visit, too, taught me many things.

I have a somewhat olive complexion and dark hair, features not out of the ordinary in my part of the world. In fact, in most of the places I've traveled to, I am unremarkable and can easily disappear in a crowd. In North Africa, however, I was a marked man, easily standing out as a foreigner. Plus, it didn't help that my friends were pasty white, one a redhead and the other a blonde. Despite being crowned as the "most swarthy" of the group, as my friends kept teasing me, I still felt as if I were "the other," with all eyes on us, scrutinizing and judging. I was acutely aware for the first time in my life that I was an outsider and part of a cultural minority. The sensation I had, I remember thinking, was likely similar to what other so-called minorities must feel while traveling to other parts of the world.

The conversation I had with the guide—indeed the whole trip to Morocco—made me self-aware in a strange way, as if I were outside of myself observing my experience. I felt as if my sense of self was but one of many senses of self that exist in this world, not one of which is superior to any other. Of course, we learn in grade school that there are varieties of experiences and cultures in the world. But that was my first experience of actually knowing it to be true. It was my first experience understanding that the "Western way" was but one way. Of course, I thought I knew this truth before those cool nights in the Moroccan desert, but it took that conversation to make it a real, concrete fact. I felt as if I overcame what it meant to be me, culturally speaking, as I tried to understand and negotiate another worldview, experience, and perspective.

This is why studying abroad can be so valuable. And this is what is meant when study abroad advocates state that the experience of studying abroad for a lengthy period of time helps you "transcend the self." You realize that there are other individuals and other cultures in the world that are no more or less important, true, and beautiful than the one from which you come. The student abroad, as McEvoy tells us, can become cosmopolitan and liberated "from those unconscious ties which have limited his identity and, in a sense, his intellectual and perceptual movement." Traveling and studying abroad liberates you from "the parochialism of one's origins."

The important point here, indeed a point that I've been alluding to throughout this book, is that the simple act of traveling to a new country will not necessarily result in your growing, transforming, or "transcending the self." Crossing a border does not instantaneously give you the qualities of being worldly or cosmopolitan. Travel does not give anyone any special qualities, abilities, or insights by default. All of that takes time, effort, and reflection.

A literal transcendence occurs when you uproot, move across continents, and implant yourself in a new environment. You must engage with, try to understand, and reflect on cross-cultural experiences in order to grow interiorly and cultivate meaning from the experience. The narrow-minded traveler—the one that constantly compares everything foreign to his "superior" home culture and way of life—fails to create a meaningful transcendence, perhaps through ignorance or bigotry.

Traveling is learning about the self just as much as it is learning about new cultures. We travel not just to explore and experience the other, but to explore and understand oneself and one's place in the world. Regardless of where in the world you visit, you always travel with yourself. I am not only referring to the physical self, your physical body, but to the conscious self, the inner workings of your mind. As the saying goes, "everywhere you go, there you are." Thus, if the point of travel is to experience new cultures, that is to understand the world better, then those who travel in body but not in mind do not really travel at all. In other words, one who travels the world but does not try to learn about the world and one's place in it is perhaps doing it wrong.

Self-awareness is not something that a traveler automatically acquires abroad. It is not a passport stamp, a mere indicator of a traveler's comings and goings. It is also not a souvenir, an easily and cheaply acquired knickknack that one soon forgets about. Self-understanding and self-transcendence are things that must be cultivated, constantly explored, and developed. Self-awareness requires a degree of self-reflection.

HOW TO REFLECT ON YOUR EXPERIENCES ABROAD

To be sure, studying abroad gives an opportunity for deeper, more critical, and more nuanced perspectives about the world to develop. But it also gives the opportunity for self-discovery. It is difficult to learn about yourself without contemplation and reflection, both of which require a certain degree of solitude, space, and time. Studies have shown that there is a correlation between students who study abroad and an interest and ability to think about oneself, the world, and one's place in it. An easy way for someone to get into the habit of contemplation and reflection while traveling is to journal.

Journaling is the window into reflective thought. And writing is the commitment of thought. Or, you can think of it like the flesh of the soul, the materiality of an idea. Journaling makes the experience real in ways merely thinking about it cannot.

Consider writing privately, in a manner closed off to the critical eyes of others, like in paper journal. Online journals—blogs—are okay, but they are public and subject to scrutiny in ways that your private thoughts are not. Plus, do you really want others to read about your rants?

Purchase a journal prior to studying abroad. Yes, even if you are a man. Purchase a sturdy hardback journal that can fit inside a small bag. Take it with you everywhere. Make it one of your goals to write in your journal every day about your thoughts, feelings, and experiences. Remember that the word "journal" comes from the French word that literally means "daily." So, commit to spending a few moments every day reflecting on the day to come and the day that just passed. It does not take that much time or effort.

Travel journals can help us explore three main areas:

- *The self.* Journaling helps you learn about yourself, your moods and behaviors, your interests and patterns.
- *Your culture.* Journaling helps you learn about the culture from which you come. It helps you identify and explore assumptions you share with others from your country.
- *The other.* Journaling helps you explore, learn about, and understand other people, other cultures, and the broader world.

Journaling also has the benefit of giving you a record of your day-to-day experiences. You will be able to return to your old journals and visit your past, younger self. It will help you understand yourself as a young traveler, what was occupying your mind at the time, your fears, aspirations, and dreams.

Writing helps your mind in ways nothing else can, especially if you dedicate a few moments each day to the practice. One approach would be to get in the habit of writing each morning. Instead of reaching for your phone in the morning, grab a cup of coffee and your journal. Start writing down what your plans are for the day, what you did on the previous day, or whatever else comes to mind. It doesn't have to be much. You can write a few lines or a few pages. The point is to document the nuances of your experiences, perceptions, and memories that will otherwise be lost to oblivion.

Journaling is also a way to connect more deeply with yourself in the present. What avenues of growth will you have if you do not reflect upon your experiences? As Socrates said, "An unexamined life is not worth living." Holidaymakers who pass through a country and do not take time to reflect on their experiences have little opportunity for growth. Had I not journaled about my embarrassment in the Moroccan desert, that lesson might have been lost on me.

REFLECT

1. How will you remember your experiences? Do you plan to write in a physical journal or do it digitally in a blog? Photography?
2. What topics could you write about?
3. When is a good time for you to commit writing a few lines or paragraphs each day?
4. Consider bringing with you a study journal, one like those made by Rhodia, Moleskine, and Leuchtturm1917. They are pricey, but they are sturdy and will last a lifetime. For a list of recommended journals, visit: https://studyabroadinstitute.org/students/journals

"Home is within you, or home is nowhere at all."

— Hermann Hesse, *Siddhartha*

19. HOME BASHING

It was the middle of January, midway through my first year abroad, and a series of dilemmas would begin to alter the course of my future. No sooner had I bought a ticket to fly to Barcelona to reconnect with some old friends than I received an email from a former colleague about a job opening in Florida. "Just apply for it," he said. "It'll be good practice for when you are ready to enter the job market."

"But, what if I get the job?" I asked. I had already committed to spend another year in Spain, this time teaching English in a high school in Madrid instead of Seville. But getting the job would force me to step down and move back to Florida. I had such a wonderful time in Spain that I was having doubts about what would otherwise have been an easy decision.

"That won't happen," my friend said. "But if it does, wouldn't it be better than getting six hundred euros a month teaching English to high schoolers?"

He had a point. I had not even finished my PhD. Heck, I had not even finished one chapter of my dissertation. There was no reason to believe that a hiring committee would even consider someone like me for the job. I was confident—and so was my friend—that there was no way that I would ever get hired. So, for the next few weeks I focused my energies on the application. I submitted all my documents in good faith and went on my way.

Days passed, then weeks. I forgot about the job and began psyching myself up over the prospect of spending another year in Spain. This time, I thought, I would be closer to the archives in which I needed to spend my time to finish my dissertation, to say nothing of being in a vibrant city, a city that not only glistened and shimmered with high cultural activity but also was smeared with a gritty urban realism. I was looking forward to the concerts, cooler weather, and pace of the capital city. I was being drawn to the lights and bustle of Madrid, a big and noisy city, in which I felt at home and at peace, and my attention was trained on fantasizing about all the opportunities the city would give me.

Then, one day, I received an email from human resources at the school I applied to, inviting me to an interview. The interview was scheduled in two weeks, in Florida, and on the same day as my trip to Barcelona.

Shit.

"It'd be good practice," my friend said to me. "Sure, the plane ticket will be costly. But just do the interview. Who knows? Maybe you'll get the job."

I decided to burn my tickets to Barcelona and bought a last-minute and expensive ticket to Florida. My two sleepless days in Florida went by, predictably, in a blur. Before I knew it, I was back in Seville. Soon I received another email from the school. It was an offer for a full-time, tenured job as a professor.

"Lucky dog," my friend said after I told him the good news. "I guess it did happen! And now you'll be making the equivalent of six hundred euros every two weeks instead of every month while also working four times as much for it!"

※

The college was a few hours away from my childhood home, in a city I had lived in for about five years as an older adult. My classmates and friends were happy for me, as I hadn't yet finished my PhD, and I had a job offer in hand. My dissertation director was also elated, as he knew how difficult the job market was, especially during the financial crisis that had been rocking the world economy.

So, a year after I unpacked my bags for the first time living in a foreign country, I found myself packing them up to leave. My professors, family, and friends reminded me that I was fortunate to have this opportunity, and that it was time to take the next step as a professional educator.

Repatriating to Florida from Spain turned out to be difficult and strange. I had my family, a group of friends, and a secure job. Though I had everything that could possibly make someone happy, something seemed off. In fact, after a few months on the job, I was profoundly unhappy and skeptical that I had made the right decision.

When I wasn't teaching or writing my dissertation, I reminisced about my time in Spain and told myself that I'd move back once I finished my PhD. I hated the fact that I needed to drive everywhere and cringed every time "Florida man" appeared on the news.

Living in Spain gave me the perspective that Florida was a land in which poor drivers, traffic jams, and urban sprawl thrived. I saw Florida as a sprawling hellscape of gated communities, strip malls, and parking lots.

I fantasized about Europe. I had dreams in which I was living in Spain doing mundane things like going to grocery stores and walking alone in the streets. It was as if my mind, my dreams, and my aspirations were still in Spain, but my body happened to be in Florida, operating almost mechanically. I felt like I no longer belonged in Florida, despite having spent much of my adult life living in the state. I felt as if I had changed, developed, and progressed, but Florida had remained firmly in place, progressing slowly or, rather, I was convinced, regressing. I loathed living in Orlando.

※

I am not a mental health professional, but in hindsight, some of my symptoms sound terribly like I was in a dark, depressive state. I spent a lot of time not only thinking about the ways in which I could have better spent my time in Spain but also regretting my decision to move back to Florida. *I should have gone to Madrid*, I often thought. I was overworked, resentful, and depressed. In my case, I never experienced any real sensation of homesickness while I was in Spain. Instead, the only symptoms of sickness arose when I went back to Florida. Someplace else had become my home.

I now realize that my sensations of depression, regret, and resentment after a long-term study abroad experience are quite common. I also now realize that it can be just as hard to *come* home as it is to *leave* home.

It is often the case that participants in study abroad programs return with a wealth of positive experiences and insights. But as the dust settles after returning home, it is not unusual for them to enter an extended period of reflection and nostalgia for their time abroad. They feel "blue," want to return abroad, and have internalized regrets. They even realize the strong relationships they had prior to leaving have changed. These sensations are known by terms like "post study abroad depression" and "reverse culture shock."

Just like the kind of culture shock that appears when an individual moves to a new place, an individual can experience culture shock when returning home. And it follows along the same kind of progression. For example, students are often excited to return home after studying abroad (the "honeymoon" phase). But that excitement soon sours. They turn more critical of their home culture and more judgmental, frustrated, and resentful until they adapt and accept. Like normal culture shock, reverse culture shock can also take some time to run its course. And that's exactly what happened with me. It took a few years, but I eventually appreciated Florida again.

Understand that it is perfectly normal to experience reverse culture shock. There are a variety of resources online to help you readjust to life back home. They—not surprisingly—involve some of the same strategies that help you deal with the initial culture shock of moving abroad. I invite you to reread the section above that deals with culture shock and apply the techniques for adjustment to your life back home.

IN CLOSING

I promised that I would give you some tips and ideas on how to get the most out of your study abroad experience. I hope that you were able to find some value and insight from the anecdotes and stories above. In closing, however, allow me to summarize the central ideas within this short book.

- Participate in a long-term study abroad program if you can. If you can't, even short-term programs are transformative.
- Travel is work. Do not always expect your study abroad experience to be an amazing adventure full of peak experiences.
- Plan to have a full set of CHASE experiences:
    - Engage with the culture.
    - Cultivate healthful habits.
    - Prioritize your academic studies.
    - Have a social life.
    - Express your creativity.
- Articulate a clear set of intentions and SMART goals for your time abroad.
- Culture shock is common. You can overcome it.
- Keep your body and mind healthy while abroad.
- Don't get distracted by what's happening back home.
- Balance work and play.

"Why do you go away? So that you can come back. So that you can see the place you came from with new eyes and extra colors. And the people there see you differently, too. Coming back to where you started is not the same as never leaving." — Terry Pratchett, *A Hat Full of Sky*

- Make local friends.
- Spend less time with people from your home culture than with locals.
- Learn the language.
- Push your limits, try new things, and get uncomfortable.
- Get to know your local environment.
- Keep a journal.

We love hearing about students' adventures studying abroad, so please reach out to us if you've found this book helpful. We would love to hear from you about your experiences! Also, if you have insights or tips that could help others, please let us know what they are, and we will be happy to consider including them in future editions of this book.

Study Abroad Institute
https://studyabroadinstitute.org
info@studyabroadinstitute.org

Part Five
Appendix

Below you will find a series of brief notes on questions and topics that concern students thinking about studying abroad. But, remember that I cannot answer your questions for you. Only you can answer them for yourself, as everyone has distinct backgrounds and contexts. The notes below will help you think about the questions that you may have and help you answer them.

20. MONEY MATTERS

HOW DO I PAY FOR STUDYING ABROAD?

Studying abroad is expensive. Fortunately, there are many programs and scholarships available to support international education. A simple Google search will result in many options like the Gilman, Fulbright, Boren, and Bailey Scholarships. Various organizations offer scholarships too. For more information, search for CEA (Cultural Experiences Abroad), CCIS (College Consortium for International Studies), CIEE (Council on International Educational Exchange), and AIFS (American Institute for Foreign Studies). Search far and wide.

If you are planning on participating in a long-term study abroad program, check your university's website for scholarship opportunities specifically designed for study abroad students at your institution. Your school also might have a dedicated scholarship or grants office that helps students search and apply for them.

Don't forget to check the various independent organizations in your community, like Rotary International and religious institutions, to see if they have any scholarships or opportunities for international education. Take advantage of these resources.

Study abroad scholarships often have deadlines well in advance of the actual study abroad dates, so it pays to begin planning sooner rather than later. Minority students often have additional scholarship opportunities, so search for those if you qualify. It also helps to apply to as many scholarships as possible.

IN-COUNTRY FINANCES

Money management is a real issue for study abroad students, most of whom will be strapped for cash. It is important to budget your money so that you do not overspend. Overspending is a particularly dangerous hazard while studying abroad, as international travelers on student visas are usually barred from any kind of employment.

Most of what I report below is illegal in practice. I am not recommending or encouraging that you engage in any of the activities that I write below, as it could jeopardize your ability to continue studying in the country and get you in serious legal trouble; I'm merely reporting what others have reported doing in the past.

Foreign students have reported making money under-the-table while abroad. Specifically, they have reported making money by teaching private English lessons. Of course, this presupposes that they were studying in countries whose national language is not English. In Spain, many of my American friends said they taught private English classes to middle school and high school students, charging their parents around fifteen euros an hour per student and giving discounts to groups of two or more. What they charged depended on their qualifications, where they lived, and how good they were at advertising and marketing. They often taught private language lessons in the client's home, a practice that rarely presented issues but did involve some risks (they vetted their clients). Likewise, the costs that they incurred traveling to and from their client's home came out of their pockets.

Other students reported working in bars, nightclubs, and hostels. Some said that they led English-language tours for tourists visiting the city.

Again, I do not recommend that you break the law. Working under-the-table is illegal in most countries. You will be in serious legal trouble if you break the law. Fortunately, there are legal alternatives like teaching online.

TEACHING ONLINE & FREELANCE WORK

If you already have a bachelor's degree or are a graduate student studying abroad, as nearly 12 percent of all US study abroad students were during the 2016–17 academic year, you have another option. And that is to teach English online to Chinese students using platforms like VIP Kid. They typically require teachers to have a bachelor's degree, a reliable internet connection, and a good showing in the online interview, but if you can get established, you'd be able to make around $20 per hour teaching virtually. In fact, many so-called "digital nomads" teach English online to help fund their lives abroad. Some make as much as $2,000 a month, but that will be time-consuming. If you have the time, patience, and interest in teaching English abroad to young Chinese students, explore whether or not online platforms like VIP Kid are right for you.

If you have special skills, consider offering your services as a freelancer on online platforms like fiverr.com and upwork.com. For example, you could edit papers remotely, translate documents, or create graphics.

REFLECT

1. Do a preliminary search for scholarships. If you believe you qualify for some, write down the names of the awards, the scholarship amounts, and the deadlines. Also, list any specific requirements they have, if any.
2. Contact your school and see if there is an office that helps secure student scholarships and grants. If so, ask for help searching for study abroad scholarships and write down the award names, scholarship amounts, requirements, and deadlines.
3. Research and contact local community groups (Rotary International, your religious community, etc.) to see if they offer scholarships of this nature. If not, ask them if they would be willing to help you with fundraising.
4. Do you identify with a minority group? If so, write down which groups you identify with and check if there are special scholarships available.
5. Do you have any skills that could be converted into online or remote work on platforms like fiverr.com or upwork.com?

21. STAYING SAFE

I was visiting Madrid one late winter day, and I noticed fliers posted around the city announcing that an American student studying at Carlos III University of Madrid had gone missing. His face also began popping up on my social media feeds. Friends and strangers were commenting on the social media posts, pleading that anyone with information about his whereabouts report it to the authorities. But it was all for naught as, about a week after he went missing, Austin Bice's body was found floating in the Matanzares River, which was not too far from where he was last seen.

By all accounts, Austin was a normal young man, who liked to have a good time but not to excess. He even made comments on his blog about enjoying his observations of Spaniards drinking too much and too frequently.

Despite this, some allege that he drank a little bit more than he could handle before heading out to a nightclub on the night he went missing. A bouncer even turned him away for appearing intoxicated, a detail that was confirmed by the autopsy that showed that he had a "high level" of alcohol in his system at the time of death.

What we know is that after being turned away by the bouncer, he went to eat with a friend. After eating, he said that he was going home and parted ways with his friend. That was the last time anyone saw him alive.

While there still is some mystery surrounding the details of his death, the coroner reported that he died from accidental drowning, as there were no signs of physical violence on his body.

We will never know what exactly happened to Austin. Was he pushed? Did he black out and accidentally fall into the river? What is certain, however, is that tragedies like this can happen to anyone who lets their guard down a little bit.

My friend Cathy and her girlfriends flew to Lisbon for a weekend getaway. I met up with Cathy when she returned to Seville, and she told me that she'd had a terrible experience.

"I spent the entire weekend in the American embassy. My passport was stolen," she said.

"How the hell did that happen?"

"My purse got snatched while I was eating lunch . . . I think. I didn't even notice."

Cathy and her friends were enjoying midday drinks in downtown Lisbon. And they felt safe. She wasn't a novice traveler, but she let her guard down, and thieves ran off with her purse, which contained her: passport, credit cards, identity cards, a camera, and cash.

Professional thieves can quite literally snatch a watch off of someone's wrist without being detected. And professional thieves often prowl around major tourist centers looking for easy targets. Pour a little alcohol into a tourist, who is already dazzled by a new city, and a thief has found easy prey.

The stories of Austin and Cathy illustrate that bad things happen to good people and experienced travelers. More importantly, many study abroad issues involve alcohol.

Do not misunderstand what I am saying as a polemic against going out or enjoying alcohol. In fact, alcohol is such a big part of some foreign cultures that one can argue that you'll be missing out on important facets of these cultures if you outright avoid it (of course religious, personal, academic, legal, or cultural prohibitions notwithstanding). For instance, the casual observer will note the importance of wine during workweek lunches, its presence during religious ceremonies, and its general consumption by Europeans over the age of eighteen. But, many problems that study abroad participants experience are related to alcohol in some capacity. Have fun, but be safe. If you drink, drink in moderation.

ASSESSING THE RISKS

As with anything that potentially pays high returns, there are usually risks involved. The most common type of risks to the student studying abroad are petty crimes, like theft.

Students are victims of more egregious crimes, so while the chances that a serious crime will be perpetrated on you are low, it is important not to have a false sense of security while traveling abroad.

When you decide what program you will take part in, think about the risks involved in your location. What are crime stats of your program destination? Are there common petty crimes? Can you find any data on their rates and areas of occurrence? Are there specific plazas, tourist areas, or train routes that report higher crime? What are the common health risks in your study abroad destination? Do you need special vaccinations? Are there any diseases that are common (diarrhea, mosquito-borne illnesses, etc.)? And what can you do to protect yourself against them?

Knowing this information may help you understand whether risks are real, likely, or merely perceived.

HOW DO I STAY SAFE ABROAD?

While many destinations around the world are much safer than some large American cities, common sense will help you remain safe. Here are some tips to help keep you safe abroad:

- Never go out alone at night. Think about the "buddy system," which entails being with at least one friend at all times so you can look out for one another. The more the merrier.
- Do not take valuable items with you, show them off, or leave them unattended.
- Never leave your purse or bag on top of a table or hanging from the back of a chair. Always keep it on your lap or tie a strap around your leg.
- Use common sense when a stranger approaches you, especially at bars, clubs, and concerts.
- Beware pickpockets and scammers, especially on public transportation and in places where tourists gather.

22. PACKING

You don't need to read a long chapter on what to pack, so let me just say that the best practice for any long-term international student is to pack light. You don't need three pairs of shoes, your large bottles of shampoo, or your entire wardrobe for a two-week trip.

If you're a long-term study abroad student, it may seem logical to pack more. But that advice is actually ill-advised. It may seem paradoxical to say that the longer you travel for, the fewer items you should bring. The reason being is that long-term travelers can easily purchase what they need as they need it. Toiletries? Shampoo? Conditioner? All those "just in case" things that you stuff into your bag that you will never use? Leave them behind. You can purchase what you need when you need it.

Determining what to pack depends on where you're traveling to, when you're going, and for how long. Generally speaking, limit the amount of clothes you bring. You will likely pick up some new items when you're abroad. And you don't want to be encumbered by hefty suitcases and bags.

For a packing list, visit:
https://studyabroadinstitute.org/students/packing

If the point of travel is to experience new cultures and to understand the world better, then those who travel in body but not in mind do not really travel at all.

23. PAY IT FORWARD

Have you ever stayed in a hostel? Forget about that terrible movie where travelers are seduced, drugged, tortured, and killed. While I can't guarantee seduction and drug use do not occur in hostels, I am fairly confident that you have a better chance of winning the lottery than you do of being kidnapped in one and having your organs harvested. Hostels are often open and friendly places full of young adults willing to travel, learn, and connect with others from around the world. Many hostels have common areas, kitchens, patios, and other spaces where travelers hang out and meet new people.

Hostels also often have makeshift libraries where travelers leave behind books they had been reading while traveling and pick up new ones that were left behind by others. It is not unusual to see books in many different languages and about many different subjects on the shelves of hostel libraries. Leaving behind an old book and picking up a new one is one of the special traditions for the bookish traveler, and the bookshelf is often the first place I go after checking into a new hostel. Flipping through the used books, looking at what people highlighted, and reading the notes left behind bring book nerds like me special joy, to say nothing of what I perceive to be a connection into the inner world of an unknown reader.

If you're traveling with this book, and you finish it while in a hostel or traveling abroad, I encourage you to leave it on a shelf, letting someone else learn and grow from reading these pages. Or simply gift it to a friend who is also studying abroad. While you're at it, leave them a little note in the front cover with some words of encouragement and your social media links. Maybe one day someone will thank you for changing their life . . .

Made in the USA
Las Vegas, NV
22 December 2023